RAILS TO THE RIM

Milepost Guide To The Grand Canyon Railway®

Al Richmond

Seventh Edition

Rails to the Rim   ISBN 0-933269-32-3

Cover Photo: Grand Canyon Railway No. 4960 crossing a ballast deck pile and frame bridge
at MP 55.1 in Cononino Canyon.

Published By:
Grand Canyon Railway

Cover Design By:
Sullivan Santamaria Design

Photography and Photo Copying By:
Al Richmond

Photographic Printing By:
Charles W. Suran Jr.

Production By:
GraphTech Digital & Printing

CONTENTS

DEDICATION

To the men and women of the Grand Canyon
Railway—past, present and future.

INTRODUCTION

The Grand Canyon Railway cannot be considered a simple spur line from Williams to the Grand Canyon. A panoply of inter-related events have combined to make it what it is today. This milepost guide will give the reader some insight into its history and surroundings along with a description of the points of interest to be seen along the right-of-way keyed to the railroad mileposts.

Chapter 3, the guide itself, is printed in larger than usual type so it can be easily read while the train is in motion. Each description will tell the reader about the natural or human history pertinent to that location. Read ahead and watch for anything that is of interest.

Once on the train the reader embarks on a journey which began over four billion years ago and may never end. The tracks are only sixty-four miles in length but the history of the land, nature and people covers much more. Geologic forces and erosion have shaped the land until it is what we see today but what seems so permanent will change as time passes. The geologic journey begins with the oldest formations in the bottom of the Grand Canyon and ends at Williams with the most recent activity. Northern Arizona is famous for its marvelous landscapes and the guide is keyed to several locations that highlight the best sights. Nature gives the rider a spectacular display of landforms, flora and fauna virtually impossible to duplicate. The trip begins in magnificent forests, crosses open vistas and ends at the south rim of one of Mother Earth's most spectacular natural formations.

The guide is not restricted to what is to be seen along the right-of-way. One section orients the reader to the Colorado Plateau and Grand Canyon region, a relatively small area with the most concentrated collection of National Parks and Monuments within the United States. Within these preserves lie some of the world's most spectacular scenery. People, plants and animals of the area are also discussed in separate segments. Lastly the history of the rebuilding of today's Grand Canyon Railway with detailed descriptions of the company's motive power and rolling stock adds to the narrative.

Cowboys, Miners, Presidents and Kings; the Story of The Grand Canyon Railway by Al Richmond is a complete history of the line from its beginnings through the reinaugural run on 17 September 1989 and up to the Centennial celebration in 2001. It is generally available where this guide was purchased.

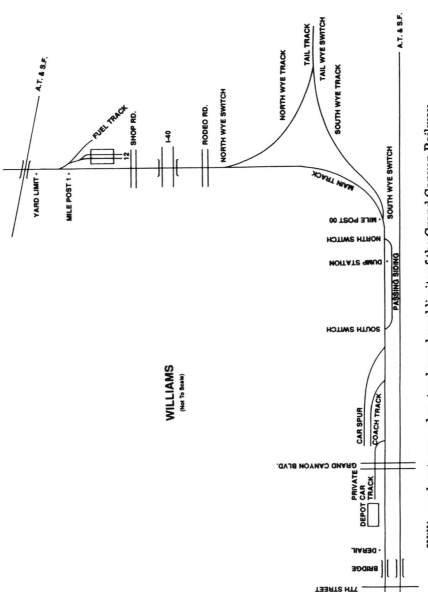

Williams depot, wye, shop tracks and yard limits of the Grand Canyon Railway.

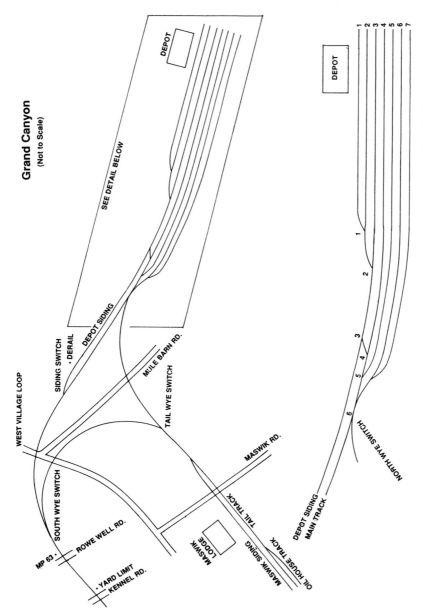

Grand Canyon
(Not to Scale)

Grand Canyon wye, yards and tracks located within the historic district of the National Park.

THE GRAND CANYON REGION

Probably the most common perception of the train trip from Williams to the Grand Canyon is of an unexceptional sixty-five mile side trip off Interstate 40. In reality this journey opens the southern door of an immense area of unparalleled and spectacular scenery on a geographical physical feature known as the Colorado Plateau.

This marvelous product of Mother Nature's best work covers 130,000 square miles in four states. Arizona and Utah have the largest share with Colorado and New Mexico not far behind. It is bordered on the south by the Mogollon Rim, at the north by the Uinta Mountains, on the west by the Wasatch Range and the Grand Wash Cliffs and on the east by the Rocky Mountains. Within these spectacular geologic features lies a high desert area which in many cases defies description for its diversity and beauty.

In order to protect, preserve and display to the people of the world the magnificent land forms of the region the government of the United States has set aside eight national parks, twenty-one national monuments, two national recreation areas, several national historic sites and millions of acres of national forests. Add to this total the dozens of state parks, the tribal park at Monument Valley and the impressive array of protected lands becomes staggering. There must be a reason for all of this and the answer is simple; some of the most beautiful and magnificent landforms in the world are here in this relatively small area.

Some of the more striking features are caused by the region's extensive areas of colorful horizontal sedimentary formations which have been uplifted, folded and fractured in such ways as to form unique landforms. Drainages cutting rapidly through these

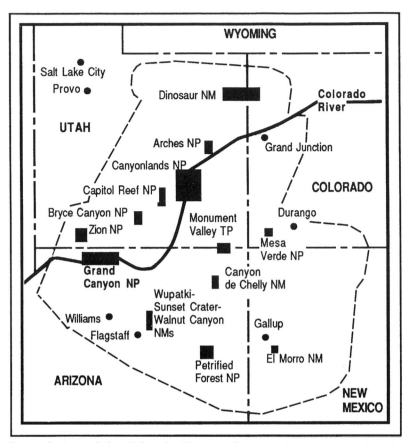

General view of the Colorado Plateau showing the locations of major cities, national parks and monuments. Not to scale.

relatively soft sedimentary layers have created deeply incised canyons with nearly vertical walls. Volcanic structures such as volcanos, cinder cones, volcanic necks, lava flows and domes intersperse and combine with the sedimentary materials to form other striking formations. These rather imposing geologic structures in this region formed a barrier which man did not penetrate to any great extent until after 1869.

In 1776 the Dominguez-Escalante expedition thoroughly crossed the region in a search for an outlet to the sea but the forbidding terrain never attracted large scale settlement. Maps produced by Don Bernardo de Miera y Pacheco from this survey clearly showed the obstacles to travel. Mormon settlement of the region began after 1850 but not until 1869 when John Wesley Powell made his famous journey of exploration down the Colorado

River did the maps of the territory begin to fill in spaces labeled *Terra Incognita*, or simply, unknown territory.

Most of the Colorado Plateau's general landmass is at an altitude of 5000 feet or higher. The greatest diversity is from the bottom of the Grand Canyon at 2000 feet to the top of the San Francisco Peaks at over 12,000 feet. Many other peaks and plateaus reach up to the ten and eleven thousand foot range.

Although the plateau is considered semi-arid and water is a constant problem for many communities, one of North America's major river systems forms the primary drainage. Over nine tenths of the Colorado Plateau is drained by the Colorado River and its many hundreds of tributaries. Almost all this water makes its way through the grandest of all canyons and every year provides thousands of people with the experience of their lives—white water rafting on the world class rapids through the Grand Canyon.

For several months out of the year many of these drainages are bone dry. In the spring runoffs from snow melt can bring these streams and rivers to flood stage with amazing rapidity. But nothing can compare with the speed with which some of these canyon drainages can fill during the annual "monsoon." The monsoon of July through September can bring considerable humidity into the region and huge thunderstorms can spring up in a matter of minutes. Flash floods are common during these times and catch the unwary traveler on the backroads and in the canyons by surprise. Imagine if you will the down-cutting of forty feet of stream bed in one storm. It happened at Kanab, Utah in 1883. If that isn't too impressive consider that two years later another storm cut the channel down another twenty-five feet. That's sixty-five feet in two years with only two storms.

Populations are centered in small communities usually with an agricultural, mining or logging history. Largest today is Flagstaff, Arizona at around 56,000 with Grand Junction, Colorado at 42,000 and Farmington, New Mexico at 40,000 next in line. Although Salt Lake City exerts considerable influence the largest community in Utah on the plateau is Price at under 10,000.

Over the years since the Mormons first began to settle the region in 1847 the land has seen a variety of uses. Initial development began with agricultural, livestock and community development. Eventually some minor industries began to appear to support the mines which developed as prospectors combed the mountains and canyons and located ore bodies. Transportation systems such as the railroads opened up other regions primarily to exploit the mineral, timber and livestock wealth. Communities sprang up overnight only to disappear with the next dawn. Boom

3

and bust created numerous ghost towns that add to the romance of the present day plateau region.

Due to the aridity of the region, the rangeland carrying capacity for cattle and sheep is low. The lushest areas will only support twenty-five cattle per square mile in the best of seasons while the more desert-like areas are overtaxed with five per square mile. Even so, summer grazing on the higher plateaus and forested areas and winter grazing on the lower plains remains a primary land use.

Today, over fifty percent of the Colorado Plateau is divided up between federal, state, county and city government functions for national parks and monuments, state, city and county lands and parks, and areas administered by the Bureau of Land Management, Forest Service and the Bureau of Reclamation. Uses for these lands include recreation, water storage, grazing, agriculture, mining, logging and administrative and maintenance facilities.

Next in size in terms of land use are the Indian reservations comprising over one third of the Plateau. Approximately fourteen tribes are located on these reservations which occur in all four of the Colorado Plateau states. Indian land uses are mostly for grazing, some agriculture, coal mining and a very small amount of light industry.

The remaining lands total only eleven percent of the total and are private holdings for residential, commercial, grazing, agricultural and industrial purposes.

Biologist C. Hart Merriam defined and described the Life Zones of North America. Of these seven life zones six are located on the Colorado Plateau and the most exaggerated difference is found within a distance of seventy miles. With the Lower Sonoran Zone below 2,500 feet at the bottom of the Grand Canyon and the Arctic-Alpine Zone on the San Francisco Peaks above 11,500 feet nearly the full range of the zones is demonstrated. Only the Arctic Zone is not present. Merriam considered this seventy miles to be representative of a trip from central Mexico to the Arctic Ocean.

All of the following zonal descriptions by general elevation are variable according to slope exposure. Zonal boundaries occur somewhat lower on north and northeast facing slopes than on warmer south and southwestern slopes.

Cactus varieties, mesquite and creosote bush characterize the flora of the Lower Sonoran Zone found on the Plateau only at the bottom of the Grand Canyon.

The flora of the Upper Sonoran Zone covers most of the Colorado Plateau region. Present between 2,500/4,000 to 7,000 feet the widest variety of plants on the Plateau occur in this zone. Sagebrush and grama grass cover much of the open areas with broken ground supporting a variety of brush including scrub live oak, salt bush and mountain ash. Juniper and pinyon occur locally in the upper reaches of this zone in many areas. Some drainages have good water supplies and support more lush vegetation including cottonwood, tamarisk, willow and other riparian species.

Forests of Douglas fir, Ponderosa pine and other pine species inhabit the Transition Zone from 6,000 to 9,000 feet. Above 7,500/8,000 feet to 9,000/9,500 feet is the Canadian Zone with its attendant fir species dominating the scene. Spruce and alpine fir species occupy the Hudsonian Zone at altitudes from 8,500/9,000 to tree line at 11,500 feet. The Canadian and Hudsonian zones are

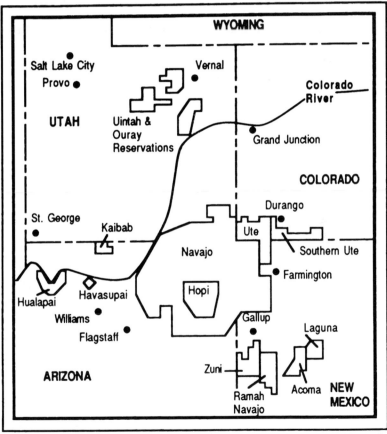

Indian reservations on the Colorado Plateau showing the general boundaries. Several smaller units of these reservations are not shown because of the small scale.

Thelma and Max Biegert, the Grand Canyon Railway principals, in front of the Grand Canyon depot just after making the public announcement on 10 January 1989 for the rebuilding of the line.

commonly combined and referred to as the Boreal Zone for they are very difficult to differentiate.

Arctic-alpine species flourish above 11,500 feet in the San Francisco Peaks area and these delineate the Arctic-Alpine Zone. The mini-plant tundra varieties along with bristle cone pine and small herbs and grasses are found here; the only location on the Plateau where they thrive.

Although much of the Plateau is bare rock and the natural saucer shape of the region dictates to a great extent the distribution of vegetation types, many fine forests flourish at the median to higher elevations. These forests are confined to the mountains and rims of the Plateau with the remainder of the area at lower elevations composed of desert or arid climate varieties of plants and grasses.

Variety best expresses the nature of climate on the Colorado Plateau. The periphery of the saucer shaped plateau receives most of the moisture with amounts exceeding twenty inches annually in some areas while the interior averages less than ten inches of precipitation throughout the year. A rain shadow caused by the high plateaus and rim deepens the aridity of the lower central areas. In contrast, several of the larger mountain systems have microclimates of their own with heavy annual precipitation.

The high elevation causes hot summers and cold winters with some areas reaching considerable extremes. Temperatures over 100°F are common in the summer with below 0°F readings frequent in the winters. Northern Arizona weather is a blend of the extreme and the comfortable but certainly not as hot as the summers in Phoenix or as cold as the winters in Colorado. Grand

One of the Baldwin KD-7 locomotives under consideration for purchase from the Chinese National Railways. GCR's CEO could not tolerate the massacre of students in Tiananmen Square and cancelled the transaction.
Max Biegert photo

Canyon and Williams weather tends to provide the visitor with a comfortable blend of changing weather patterns with extremes kept to a minimum. Summers usually sport high temperatures in the upper eighties and winters can have extended periods in the forties and fifties. Travelers should be prepared for the extremes because heavy snows and below zero temperatures are possible. Also, while one travels to and from Williams it doesn't take long for the temperatures to soar above the one hundred degree mark in July and August.

Climatic variations are largely responsible for the physical shaping of the land by frequent freezing and thawing cycles and rapidly alternating dry and wet periods. These processes also affect human occupation of the land.

The overall aridity of the region is most likely its best asset. If the prevailing climate of the area had been more humid in all probability few of the extraordinary landforms which we enjoy today could have formed and therefore no need would exist for national parks and monuments to protect the spectacular vertical scenery. Agriculture, industry and population would all have been more extensive than is now possible. As most of the lands remain in the public domain and the arid climate prevails the more spectacular features of the land are preserved reasonably well.

Riders on the Grand Canyon Railway enter into a region with immense possibilities for enjoyment. This can be the start of a vacation or many vacations with countless pleasant memories. Take the time to explore and enjoy.

At sunrise on 17 September 1989, GCRy No. 29 rests on display in front of the Williams depot. The opening day crowds have not arrived as yet and the cars of the first passenger train to the Grand Canyon in twenty-one years wait for No. 18 in front of the Fray Marcos hotel.

8

Work on locomotive No. 18 had not been completed the day before the re-inaugural run. Volunteers helped with the jobs which released engine-men for the mechanical work. Painting trim was a necessary last-minute task done by anyone who could handle a paint brush.

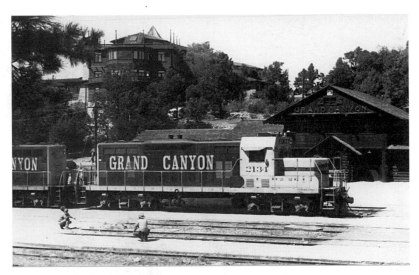

This GCRy ballast train actually made the first scheduled run on the rebuilt line from Williams to the Grand Canyon on 11 September 1989. GP-7s 2072 and 2134 wait for orders at the depot below El Tovar hotel.

By 10:00 am on the 17th of September several thousand spectators had gathered to witness the running of the re-inaugural steam train to the Cañon. A full slate of dignitaries gave testimony to the solemnity of the occasion while the Northern Arizona University marching band lent a festive air.

Over one thousand people waited for the train at the Grand Canyon depot. They witnessed another round of speeches and dedications in front of the historic depot and the driving of a golden spike.

GEOLOGY

An explanation of the geology of the region from Williams to the Grand Canyon gives an idea of the natural forces that sculpted this beautiful expanse over which the train travels. The rails follow a landscape that changes considerably over its length of sixty-five miles. Many different factors and forces combined to produce a varied and unique environment across the span of billions of years. There are very few places in this world where one can see such a magnificent diversity in so small an area. Also, the Canyon visitor gets a look back into time which covers almost half of the earth's on-going history of formation.

Most geologists place the origins of planet earth around 4.5 billion years ago. At the north end of the railroad the Vishnu Schist in the bottom of the Grand Canyon is at least two billion years old. It is a metamorphic rock which means it changed in form. The schist is believed to have been originally composed of volcanic and sedimentary rocks until heat and pressure reformed it into its present state. In this form the material is unable to be accurately dated by any known methods. However, the Zoroaster granite intrusions in the schist are dateable by a Potassium-Argon process which puts its age at 1.8 billion years. Relatively we know the schist has to be older but how much older is open to conjecture.

At the other end of the geologic spectrum and at the south end of the railroad Quaternary lava flows from very recent times predominate. The area around Williams has seen volcanic activity from four million to just a few thousand years ago. Thus we have a railroad with its anchors in the dim beginnings of time and the present geologically speaking. Between these two extremes occurred many episodes of deposition, erosion, volcanism, weathering and relocation. In a general way this guide will cover the geologic transition to explain why the land appears as it does and

11

provide the visitor with an understanding of the forces and time involved with the process.

Geologists recognize three basic groups of rocks and all are represented on the Colorado Plateau in the Grand Canyon region. Before giving a description of the different horizons (layers) that constitute this region, it will be helpful to understand something of their origin and makeup.

Sedimentary rocks have their origins in sediment from a variety of sources. Marine calcareous deposits composed of the micro-and macroscopic shells of organisms and other sea life form limestones. Eolian (wind blown) or fluvial (stream) depositions from eroded rocks make up sandstones. Mudstones and shales originate from dissolved rocks and soils transported from another location. Conglomerates are mixtures of materials which include everything from sand sized grains to large boulders. These are most commonly deposited in water environments such as seas, lakes or streams and in the case of eolian deposits, dunes. Glaciers at the top of the San Francisco Peaks also moved sedimentary material from one location to another. All are normally stratified according to age with the youngest on top.

Igneous rocks originate deep within the bowels of the earth as magma. This material is molten and arrives at the surface in a variety of means and only after penetrating the earth's crust. Most commonly this is through a long process of intrusion, uplift and erosion that brings the materials to the surface. Granite is the most widely recognized rock which goes through this process. Magma under pressure is squeezed into the crust of the earth where it slowly cools and hardens. Here it remains until pressure is exerted to force it up to the surface as in a mountain building episode. Then erosion takes over and further exposes the granite to view.

Extrusive igneous rocks such as rhyolite and basalt most commonly arrive at the surface by means of volcanos or lava flows. Molten material follows channels through the earth's crust and is rapidly cooled upon exposure to the air. These materials are seen as large rocks, lava flows, cinders, tuff or ash. Volcanos can take on several different forms and we see good examples in this region. Much of the southern half of the railroad passes through an area of volcanoes, cinder cones and lava flows.

Metamorphic rocks start out as something else and after being subjected to great heat and pressure deep within the earth's mantle they change into their present state. Then through a process of uplift, faulting and/or erosion they are exposed at the earth's surface. In the Grand Canyon tectonic uplift and erosion

ERA	PERIOD	EPOCH	AGE
CENOZOIC	Quaternary	Holocene	
			.01 my
		Pleistocene	
			1.8 my
	Tertiary	Pliocene	
			5 my
		Miocene	
			25 my
		Oligocene	
			37 my
		Eocene	
			55 my
		Paleocene	
			63 my
MESOZOIC	Cretaceous		
			135 my
	Jurassic		
			180 my
	Triassic		
			230 my
PALEOZOIC	Permian		
			275 my
	Pennsylvanian		
			330 my
	Mississippian		
			365 my
	Devonian		
			410 my
	Silurian		
			435 my
	Ordivician		
			500 my
	Cambrian		
			600 my
PRE-CAMBRIAN	Proterozoic		
			2 by
	Archeozoic		

Geologic time scale in millions (my) and billions (by) of years with all of the known time divisions in the Grand Canyon region. These ages are not absolute and adjusted as more information becomes available.

by the Colorado River have combined to expose the two billion year old Vishnu Schist. Some of the more common metamorphic rocks found in the region are quartzite, gneiss, marble and schist.

Let us begin this description of the horizons at the bottom of the Canyon and proceed upwards in the order of formation. This will take the reader from the beginnings right up to most recent times.

Vishnu Schist
Travelers on the river and those hardy souls who hike the trails or ride mules into the Grand Canyon will have an opportunity to inspect and marvel at the magnificent mass of rock which is the Vishnu Schist. Visitors looking down from the south rim will see the dark green and black walls which form the inner gorge. Light colored intrusions into the schist mark the paths molten Zoraster Granite followed through the host rock. This two-billion-year-old metamorphic formation of an unknown thickness constitutes the basement rock for all of the layers above. Originally formed in the Archeozoic Period this schist had been laid down as sedimentary limestone, sandstone and shale with lava beds interspaced before being combined under heat and pressure into its present state.

Grand Canyon Supergroup
Several colorfully layered formations across the Canyon appear out of place when viewed from the south rim. This group of Proterozoic Period shales, quartzites and limestones had been deposited between 1.2 billion and 800 million years before present and later tilted during uplifting tectonic episodes. Erosion then leveled off the upper surfaces to form what is known as the Great Unconformity. This represents almost 300 million years of missing materials whose origins cannot be determined. Remaining materials comprise a combined tilted horizon of 15,000 feet.

During the Cambrian Period the next three horizons of sandstone, shale and limestone represent varying depositional episodes in the Grand Canyon region. All of these deposits formed as an inland sea intruded into what is now a large portion of the western United States. Although each horizon is made up of different material they all progress upwards from coarse to increasingly finer grains. These three layers constitute what is referred to as the Tonto Group.

Tapeats Sandstone
As the sea moved inland the seashore environment which included dunes formed what is now a 100 to 300 foot thick horizon. What

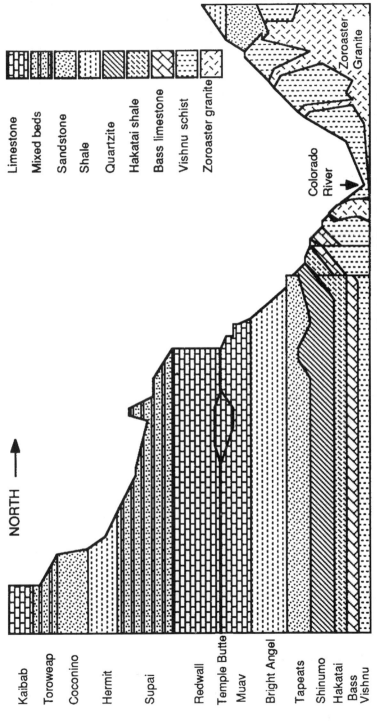

NORTH →

Limestone
Mixed beds
Sandstone
Shale
Quartzite
Hakatai shale
Bass limestone
Vishnu schist
Zoroaster granite

Kaibab
Toroweap
Coconino
Hermit
Supai
Redwall
Temple Butte
Muav
Bright Angel
Tapeats
Shinumo
Hakatai
Bass
Vishnu

Colorado
River

Zoroaster
Granite

Generalized cross section of the Grand Canyon showing most of the horizons visible from the south rim. Layers range from the two billion year old Vishnu schist at the Colorado River to the 250 million year old Kaibab limestone on the rim.

must have been a very turbulent shallow sea deposited coarse grained tan to dark brown sands along its advancing shoreline. Approximately 550 million years old, this horizon formed easily recognized cliffs directly above the dark Vishnu Schist. Due to its varying colors and uneven surface this layer has been described as looking like burned newspaper.

Bright Angel Shale

When the sea advanced the coastline continued to grow while the quieter waters further out began the process of building the 200 to 450 foot thick layer of shales above the Tapeats. Deposits of soft muds made up of clays and silts which included considerable marine life of the Cambrian Period formed the beautiful greenish slopes of the Bright Angel Shale. These approximately 540 million year old mudstones are an abundant source for the fossilized remains of trilobites, worms and brachiopods.

Muav Limestone

Another ten million years passed and the sea became deeper and with this depth came the offshore deposits that ultimately formed the 150-800 foot thick primarily limestone cliff. Layers of greyish limestones with some silt included grade up from the Bright Angel Shale. This horizon is largely composed of calcium carbonates from the exo-skeletons of microscopic marine life that filtered down to the sea floor, and other bottom dwelling life forms such as brachiopods.

Reference to the geologic time scale indicates the following periods as the Ordivician and Silurian (500-410 million years before present). Evidence of these two divisions of time are unknown in the Grand Canyon region. They represent a time when the land appeared from under the retreating sea and began a process of erosion. Another unconformity exists here in that nothing remains to show any depositional episodes nor can it be determined to what depth the Muav had grown. Obviously some limestone has been removed because the Temple Butte limestone rests in channels carved in the Muav by erosional streams.

Temple Butte Limestone

A reddish, greyish or purplish horizon forming cliffs anywhere from 100 to 1000 feet in thickness. When seen from the south rim this horizon is relatively thin and usually difficult to detect. It is most easily recognized in lenses carved into the Muav. This Devonian Period limestone is approximately 370 million years old and contains fossils of some long extinct armored fishes. After the

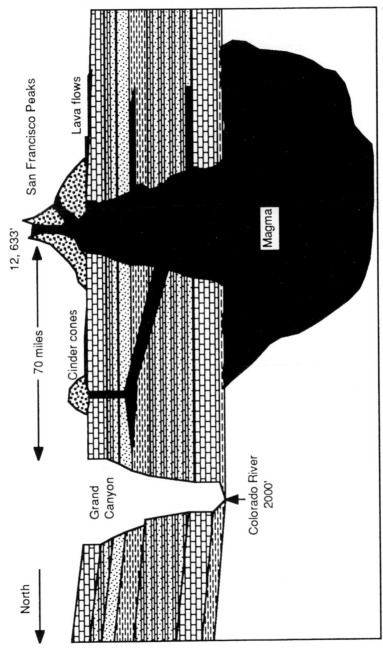

Generalized cross section of the Colorado Plateau showing the region from the San Francisco Peaks to the Grand Canyon which represents a horizontal distance of seventy miles and a vertical distance of more than 10,600 feet.

North

San Francisco Peaks

Lava flows

12, 633'

70 miles

Cinder cones

Grand Canyon

Colorado River 2000'

Magma

long erosional period which preceded it, the warm seas returned once again to the region and began the excruciatingly slow process of deposition and conversion to dolomite.

Oceans in modern times have a depositional rate of approximately three feet for every 7500 years. Deposition of shales and sandstones can occur at the rates of three feet for every 3000 and 1500 years respectively.

Redwall Limestone

Probably the most easily recognized formation, these 400 to 650 foot thick red cliffs form the upper part of the middle limestone band in the Grand Canyon. At approximately 330 million years of age these Mississippian Period layers of limestone contain one of the most abundant assemblages of fossils. Crinoids, corals, brachiopods, bryozoans, mollusks, foraminifera and trilobites all resided in the warm, shallow sea overlying this region and contributed their carbonate shells to the continuous process of deposition. Limestone is naturally grey as is the Redwall, but red stain carried down by rainwater from the overlying Hermit Shale and Supai Formation gave the horizon its distinctive color and name.

Supai Group

This 600 to 700 foot thick sloping horizon is actually made up of four separate depositional episodes and materials. The lower three are from the Pennsylvanian and the upper unit is of the Permian Period. Generally considered about 300 million years old, this group represents deposits in a shore and marginal marine environment of limestone, shale, red siltstone and light red to tan sandstone indicating a fluctuating condition of transgression and regression of a shallow sea. This swampy environment produced the Watahomigi, Manakacha and Wescogame Formations and the Esplanade Sandstone from bottom to top. Fossilized plants contained in the beds confirm the changing environments.

Hermit Shale

Also Permian in age this approximately 275 million year old horizon provides one of the more outstanding contrasts visible from the south rim. At a thickness of 300 feet this dark red slope appears at the foot of the brightly contrasting Coconino Sandstone and above the much lighter Esplanade Sandstone. Closely related to the Supai Group in depositional environment the pigments contained in its siltstones wash down onto the Redwall Limestone with the results described above. Mud cracks and plant fossils establish an origin in swampy lagoons.

Coconino Sandstone

Ranging from 50 to 300 feet in thickness this bright tan crossbedded sandstone forms a sharp vertical wall between two slopes. At 270 million years this Permian Period horizon gives evidence of the rapidly changing environments of the times. These crossbeds are the product of a very dry eolian (windy) environment that gave birth to mammoth dunes. If one cut into a modern sand dune the same type of lines would be seen as evidenced in this formation. These dunes covered northern Arizona and southern Utah in what can only be compared with the modern Sahara Desert. No fossilized remains of any animal life other than the tracks of small reptiles have been found.

Toroweap Formation

Another Permian Period formation, this 200 foot thick 260 million year old horizon indicates another change in the environment. A marine transgression and regression accounts for the tan limestone and sandstone found on the Toroweap slopes and ledges. Interbedding of gypsum, which is an evaporite, is common in this formation. Wide varieties of marine fossils such as Bryozoans, corals and mollusks give testimony to the life forms that flourished during these changes.

Kaibab Limestone

The visitor to the south rim looking down into the great abyss is standing on Permian age Kaibab Limestone. At 300 feet in thickness this 250 million year old horizon constitutes the actual north and south rim of the Grand Canyon. Slightly sandy in content, this limestone resulted from deposits made in a warm, shallow sea which returned after leaving the Toroweap. Fossilized crinoids, sponges and brachiopods are abundant in this formation. After exposure to the elements occurred, this horizon has experienced some surface erosion.

The sea responsible for the Kaibab also made additional deposits no longer found on the rim. Tens of millions of years of sediments are missing from the Permian/Triassic Period time and constitute yet another unconformity. Remnant younger red sediments of the Triassic Period Moenkopi Formation are seen south of the Canyon capped with basaltic lava. Virtually all of this formation above the Kaibab Plateau has been eroded into oblivion. Probably much of the Moenkopi underwent severe fracturing during the radical uplift of the Plateau during the Laramide Orogeny of the late Cretacious to early Tertiary and became easy prey to the erosional rain waters. Literally there is little or no evidence of Jurassic or younger depositions until the late Pliocene Epoch.

Certainly by now the visitor has been appropriately impressed by the diversity and magnitude that defines the Grand Canyon. Natural forces have formed all of these magnificent layers over a period of billions of years and presented them in such precise and varying layers just to visually delight the Holocene tourist. Understanding the processes that created these various horizons is not all that difficult. But what forces combined to present them as we see them today?

Discussion and argument between geologists about the mechanics of the formation of the Canyon has gone on for years and continues to this day. Many might think a simple process of down-cutting by the Colorado River gave us this magnificent gorge. Current theory is divided but geologic evidence seems to favor one which gives us a very plausible but unproved answer.

During Tertiary times the ancestral Colorado River, a small stream by today's standard, wended its way out of what is now Colorado, into Utah and then into Arizona. The Kaibab Upwarp formed by the Laramide Orogeny blocked its western path and it turned south into eastern Arizona and formed the ancient and vanished Lake Bidahochi. At the same time a drainage system to the west moved steadily eastward across the plateau by a process called headward erosion. This process, evidenced in the many areas of the country effected by arroyo cutting, eventually cut its way through the Kaibab Upwarp and captured the Colorado River and gave it an outlet to the sea.

The Rio Colorado, a name given to it by Spanish explorers for its reddish-brown silt-laden waters, is indeed a mighty river by any stretch of the imagination. When Don Garcia Lopez de Cardeñas, one of Coronado's conquistadores, looked down into the Grand Canyon in 1540 he saw what he believed to be a stream no wider than six feet. Had he reached the river he would have found the great distance from which he viewed it had distorted his perspective. For many years the Colorado remained a barrier to exploration and not until 1776 did Franciscan explorers actually cross the river and report its true scale. Before being robbed of its contents by all of the states lining its banks, the once wild and mighty Colorado delivered its silt-laden waters to the Gulf of California over a 1440 mile course with its origins in the Rocky Mountains of Colorado. This transit also has a vertical drop of over nine thousand feet, averaging more than six feet per mile. Its drainage system covers approximately 260,000 square miles in

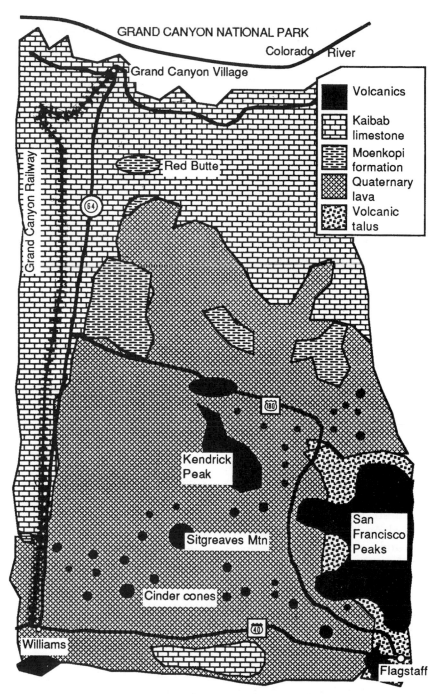

Williams-Grand Canyon-Flagstaff area showing volcanics, remnant Moenkopi formation, lava flows and Kaibab limestone.

seven states and Mexico and includes nearly all of the 130,000 square mile Colorado Plateau.

Today, its waters are impounded behind many dams and siphoned off for agricultural and power use and to provide water for the populations of many cities and towns. This once free and mighty river which conquered and crossed more mountains than any river in the United States today is reduced to a shallow, brackish stream by the time it reaches Yuma on the Arizona/ Mexico border. But occasionally nature delivers an overabundance of precipitation in the river's watersheds and engineers underestimate the runoff which in turn overtaxes storage capacity of the dams. During these times the Colorado again reminds us of its magnificent power by effortlessly pushing aside man's puny efforts at control. The river is still there and so are the changes that effect the shape of the Canyon.

The side canyons began to form through a series of ongoing processes involving continued tectonic uplift, rapid downcutting of relatively soft materials by the river, and erosion by freezing and thawing and wind and water. As one looks into the Canyon it is easy to see that the canyons on the north side of the river are more extensive than those of the south. When the Kaibab Upwarp rose about 5000 feet above its original position it did not do so uniformly. The Kaibab Plateau to the north of the river rose higher than the Coconino Plateau to the south. This formed a southerly slope and drainages therefore flowed primarily from north to south. Most of the precipitation that falls on the 8000' north rim of the Canyon flows toward the Colorado River while most on the 6800' south rim flows away from the river. These streams drain south and disappear into the faults and channels of the Kaibab Limestone or are captured by other drainages with eventual terminuses at the Colorado outside the National Park.

Faulting also contributes to the erosion of the side canyons by cutting across the formations and providing a channel for water to flow. The Bright Angel Fault provided a route for water erosion to carve out an access from the south and north rims to the river. The Bright Angel Trail drops down into the Canyon just to the west of the train station, passes through Indian Gardens and across the river on one of two suspension bridges to Phantom Ranch where it begins to follow Bright Angel Creek up the North Kaibab Trail to the north rim for a total distance of twenty-two miles.

During the southbound trip riders can see Kaibab limestone outcrops all of the way from the rim to Valle. Reddish soils cover much of the terrain which in many places has high concentrations of remnant eroded Moenkopi sandstone. This holds true during the descent from the south rim at 6800 feet to Valle at 5800 feet and continues for a few miles as the train begins the climb back up to Williams.

Here evidence of volcanic action appears in the form of lava flows and random volcanic rocks all of the way into Williams. The tracks rise and fall over a series of younger and younger lava flows interspaced by more and more frequent cinder cones. Views to the west and east are filled with volcanic peaks rising from a couple of thousand to over six thousand feet above track level.

During a period of time from fifteen million until less than a thousand years ago volcanoes in this area spewed ash, cinders and volcanic bombs into the air and unleashed lava flows across the landscape. The oldest features are to the west of Williams and the youngest to the east. Origins of Bill Williams Mountain have been dated at four million years ago. The San Francisco Peaks are the youngest major feature on the horizon. Just beyond them to the east is found Sunset Crater National Monument. For all practical purposes the eruption which produced this cinder cone and lava flow occurred just a few seconds ago in geologic time. This event is dated around 900 years before present and the resulting formations are really worth the visit. Here the visitor is treated to almost pristine examples of a variety of volcanic activities that have just begun the evolutionary process of forestation.

The San Francisco Peaks are worthy of separate discussion. It is a stratovolcano and came into being through a series of volcanic eruptions dating from 1.8 million to two hundred thousand years ago. Humphrey's Peak at 12,633 feet is the highest point in Arizona and is just one of the peaks on this mountain. Agassiz Peak at 12,356 feet is also part of the mountain and these two are the only peaks in Arizona over 12,000 feet. The peaks ring the inner basin, a collapsed caldera formed when the mountain blew out to the east in an episode very similar to that exhibited by Mount St. Helens in 1980. If an extrapolation of the slopes is continued upward until they intersect, an original peak of well over 15,000 feet is found to be possible. This would have made the mountain higher than any other in the continental United States. During several of its active periods lava flows which cover more than three thousand square miles have originated from the mountain.

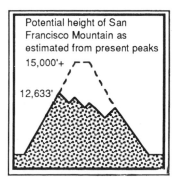

Potential height of San Francisco Mountain as estimated from present peaks

15,000'+

12,633'

23

Snow caps this beautiful mountain up to ten months out of the year. This is not so surprising when one understands the inner basin and exterior slopes once hosted at least two episodes of glaciers in the Pleistocene Epoch. Glacial moraines are easily visible on the inner slopes and floor of the basin. Evidence of glacial activity is also found on the outer slopes but it is not so obvious. Winter skiing at the Snow Bowl resort lures many denizens from the desert valleys to the south. Summer visitors can ride the ski lifts up to the 11,000 foot level on Mt. Agassiz where the view encompasses a one hundred mile panorama to include all of the terrain crossed by the Grand Canyon Railway.

Today we live on a land which has undergone many changes and will continue to change. What is chronicled here is but the beginnings of what is yet to come. A future visitor to the region will very likely see something entirely different than what we see now. We know environments and landforms change but we can only guess as to what the future holds in store for the Grand Canyon.

Grand Canyon Railway Alco FPA-4 diesel locomotive No. 6776 stands ready to depart Williams Depot with the *Williams Flyer* to the Grand Canyon. This is one of five FPA-4s that GCR purchased from VIA, the Canadian passenger railroad. They were completely overhauled and painted in the GCR shops with the distinctive livery of the railway.

The Grand Canyon Railway day begins with a Wild West show. Every morning the Marshall faces off with the world famous Cataract Creek Gang. These notorious desperadoes are dealt swift Western justice but always seem to reappear to rob the afternoon train from the Canyon.

GCR *Williams Flyer* departing the depot with the only operable A-B-B-A Alco set in the country. The FPA-4s are diesel engines with cabs for the crew and the FPB-4s are without cabs

GCR No. 18 at the Bright Angel overlook. This Alco steam engine is a consolidation type, 4-8-0 built in 1910. It has been completely rebuilt in the GCR shops at Williams. No. 18 ran the first train to the Canyon during the reinaugural on 17 September 1989.

GCR No. 29 is the second steam locomotive to enter service with the GCR. Built by Alco in 1906 it is also a consolidation type 2-8-0 and is the line's oldest locomotive.

GCR No. 4960 is the youngest steam locomotive on the roster. Built by Baldwin in 1923, it is a Mikado type 2-8-2. This powerful locomotive is arguably the most extensive rebuild using modern steam technology in the United States. All work was accomplished at the GCR shops.

Nos. 29 and 4960 double-headed at Imbleau station, milepost 52. More than one locomotive is used when the train length exceeds the limits of a single unit. The GCR commonly uses more than one unit in combinations of steam and/or diesel.

GCR coach car No. 2153 with a happy load of passengers on the way to the Canyon. The Pullman Company built these Harriman style coaches in 1923 for the Southern Pacific Railroad and rebuilt by GCR to Pullman specifications in 1989.

The GCR *Cafe Car*. Built in 1952 by Budd, this stainless steel car operated on the Pennsylvania RR as a parlor drawing room and rebuilt for food service with the Penn Central and Amtrak. GCR acquired her in 1998.

GCR deluxe observation dome car, *Grand View*. It arrived on the GCR in 2004 after a long history beginning in 1948 on the Burlington Route in *California Zephyr* service and with several other railroads to include one each in Mexico and Canada.

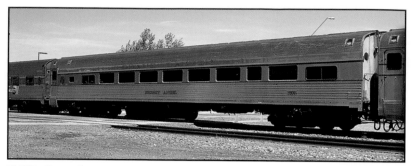

GCR first class car *Bright Angel*. Budd built this luxury coach car in 1952 for the Pennsylvania RR and it was used on the *Congressional* and *Senator* trains. It later served the Penn Central and Amtrak before coming to GCR in 2003.

GCR luxury class parlor car *Chief*. Built by Budd for the Atlantic Coast Line's *Champion* trains in 1947. It later moved to Amtrak in 1971 and then into charter service in Texas & Mexico. The platform was added in 1999 and it arrived at GCR in 2002.

A string of GCR cars waiting to enter the shops for refurbishing. Fourteen of these are newly acquired CalTrain coach cars to supplement the aging 1923 fleet of GCR coaches.

Grand Canyon Railway's annual holiday *Polar Express* thrills children and parents alike. Nightly train rides to the North Pole and a chance to visit with Santa Claus create the family memories that will be treasured forever.

GCR's newest F40FH diesels are former Amtrak F40PH 3000 HP units. Built by EMD in 1979 No. 239 came to GCR in 2004. Seen here with the *Canyon Limited*, its distinctive livery blends perfectly with the first, deluxe, and luxury class cars on this inaugural run.

GCR No. 29 as it rolls out of the shop in 2004 after a two year major rebuilding which included the latest steam technology. This powerful 2-8-0 is well suited to the curves and grades of the Grand Canyon line.

MILEPOST GUIDE

Milepost marker 5 is visible on both the north and south side of the post to the east side of the train.

Mileposts are markers much like those seen on highways set out by the railroad to tell distances. The markers are on wooden 4 X 4 posts about eight feet high set out on the east side of the right-of-way. Markers are visible on both sides of the posts and read from south to north starting at the first turnout to the Williams wye and ending at the Grand Canyon.

In this milepost guide the numbers appearing at the upper left of the following paragraphs are keyed to the mileposts. Numbers do not begin until the first turnout of the Williams wye as this is the traditional zero mileage point for the line. When the train is travelling at 30 mph a milepost is passed every two minutes. The reader can estimate the tenths of a mile by allowing about twelve seconds per tenth at this speed and adjusting if the train is moving faster or slower.

WILLIAMS DEPOT AND FRAY MARCOS HOTEL. Welcome aboard the new Grand Canyon Railway. Your train is spotted in front of the historic Fred Harvey hotel and Santa Fe depot. The AT&SF Railway Company built the hotel as part of the Fred Harvey chain of hotels and Harvey House restaurants throughout the southwest. It is named after Fray Marcos de Niza, a Franciscan friar who in 1539 started the quest for the Seven Cities of Cibola with his discoveries of what turned out to be the Zuni pueblos. When the doors of the Fray Marcos opened in March, 1908 it represented state of the art facilities and comfort for its customers. Originally the hotel opened with twenty-one rooms and later expanded with an additional twenty-two room north wing. Today it houses the Grand Canyon Railway Museum, open to the public free of charge. Plans call for the company offices to be located on the second floor. The color of the building as you see it is the original color and to determine this it became necessary to cut down through years of different colored paint layers. The company is determined to recreate the history of this railroad as accurately as is possible and the hotel and depot reflect this determination. Even the furnishings of the depot, lounge and gift shop reflect a vintage flavor. The entire structure is the largest and oldest poured concrete structure in Arizona and is on the National Register of Historic Places.

During much of the line's history this depot served as the southern terminus. Here in the station the dispatcher, station agent, telegrapher and other officials worked both the north-south and east-west rail traffic. Located to the south and east of the depot the Williams yards handled freight traffic. To the east the Santa Fe facilities included the roundhouse, shops, fueling and watering towers, section house, bunkhouse and the connection of the Grand Canyon line to the main line. North of the station the company houses served as homes to several generations of railroad workers and many are still in use today. Combined use of all of these facilities has been in effect by agreements from the time of the Santa Fe & Grand Canyon and the Santa Fe Pacific railroads.

CITY OF WILLIAMS. Founded in 1881 with the establishment of a post office on the C. T. Rogers cattle ranch Williams began to expand when the Atlantic and Pacific Railroad worked its way across northern Arizona in 1882. A&P management designated Williams as a division headquarters com-

plete with a roundhouse and the town grew into a prosperous railroad, ranching and logging community. At the turn of the century the town suffered several disastrous fires which destroyed most of the buildings. The worst occurred in July of 1901. When the train begins to move the whistle will sound for the crossing of Grand Canyon Boulevard, originally second street, and as the train crosses the street look off to the right (south) and the historic buildings of Front

Whistle board. These alert the engineer to a grade crossing which requires a whistle signal for warning.

Street come into view. These are the only original buildings that survived the fires. In the early years this street boomed twenty-four hours a day. Several restaurants (mostly Chinese) and many bars occupied the ground floors of these buildings and others long since gone. Second floor cribs and houses of ill repute operated freely for many years. When a mixture of hard working and hard playing railroaders, cowboys and loggers lubricated with a liberal supply of booze got together a volatile brew resulted. This street frequently played host to fist, knife and gun fights. The town is named after William Sherley Williams or "Old Bill" Williams as he had been known to his mountain men companions. Truly one of the old mountain men of the west his rough ways seemed to surface in his namesake town long after his passing. This crude behavior seldom flowed over into the more respectable parts of town where the merchants and families of the railroad and mill employees resided.

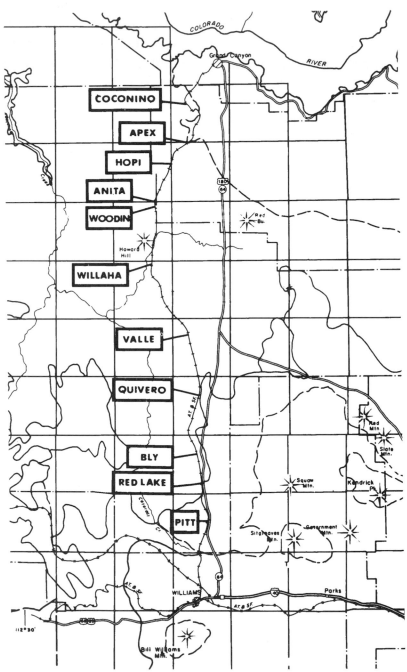

Map No. 1. The Grand Canyon Railway from Williams to the Cañon showing all of the stations.

28

Williams has seen good and bad times. The businesses of railroading and logging and ranching created a prosperous economy for the town. Mining interests for a while looked as though they would also contribute to the town's wealth and growth but failed to materialize. When motor vehicles came into common use Williams became an important stop on old Route 66. This community registered the "Gateway to the Grand Canyon" trademark because the town actually assumed that role. The town began to decline when the Saginaw and Manistee Lumber Company shut down its mill and box plant in the 1940s. Residents lost jobs and city revenues dropped considerably but when the Santa Fe main line by-passed the town and the Grand Canyon Railway shut down passenger service in the 1960s the community really began to feel the pressure. In 1984 Interstate 40 by-passed Williams and effectively sealed its fate. Visitors now witness the revival of a dying town brought back to life by a determined population and the new Grand Canyon Railway.

SITE OF FUTURE DEVELOPMENT. Just after the train crosses Grand Canyon Boulevard look off to the north. This large open area adjacent to the tracks and down to the wye will be developed into railroad facilities and attractions. Historically this area has been the site of Atlantic & Pacific Railroad, Santa Fe Pacific Railroad, and finally Atchison, Topeka and Santa Fe Railway shops, roundhouse, turntable, fueling, watering, and servicing facilities for both steam and diesel equipment.

0.0-0.3 TURNOUT FOR MAINLINE LEG OF THE WILLIAMS WYE. It became necessary to build a wye at both ends of this spur line in order to turn the trains around. The Santa Fe & Grand Canyon Railroad built the wye in Williams and the

Atchison, Topeka and Santa Fe Railway built the one at Grand Canyon. The turnout (switch) begins the main-line leg of the wye. This is actually milepost 0 for the Grand Canyon Railway. Construction of a turnout from the main line of the Santa Fe Pacific Railroad at this location marked the beginnings of the line in 1898. Because this is a spur line originating from a railroad of a different company, the milepost numbers begin at 0 and have nothing to do with those of the east-west main line. At milepost 0.3 the train will cross Rodeo Road and this is the location of the apex of the wye. As the train turns into the wye the east leg and base are visible off to the east. Good photo locations for departing trains.

0.68   INTERSTATE HIGHWAY 40. Completion of this section of the interstate marked the end of construction on the entire length of Interstate 40 which stretches from Barstow, California to Wilmington, North Carolina. This last section effectively barred much of the tourist traffic Williams had come to depend upon so heavily for a livelihood.

0.98   ENGINE AND CAR FACILITIES. On the east side of the tracks the large building is the company's new engine shop and the future site of the car yards and servicing facility. This well equipped shop is capable of handling the largest locomotives and services all of the company's steam and diesel engines and cars. New and used equipment from abandoned railroad shops such as the Union Pacific Omaha shop provides the mechanical department with a capacity to manufacture necessary parts unavailable on the market. A drop table allows removal of the running gear on engines and trucks on the rolling stock for maintenance. The mechanical department has the capability and experience to completely overhaul or rebuild a steam engine here. This includes boiler work most other shops in the country will not attempt. Cars can be completely overhauled or rebuilt as necessary to include electrical and wood work.

1.3   WILLIAMS YARD LIMIT. Grand Canyon Railway yards at Williams have a speed limit of up to twenty miles per hour. All traffic within the yards cannot exceed the restricted speed for safety reasons. The crews in the yards take care of daily business via radio communication with the dispatcher but all trains operating on the main line require written orders called track warrants. Train movements are also controlled by bulletins and instructions issued as necessary. Keep in mind this is a full time railroad and subject to all federal and state rules and regulations.

1.3   SANTA FE OVERPASS. In 1960-61 the Santa Fe Railway constructed this by-pass around the north side of Williams. Traffic through Johnson Canyon to the west of Williams with its many twists, turns, bridges and tunnels slowed main line traffic considerably. This high speed ribbon rail double track replaced the old main line through Williams. When the Santa Fe began to use the new tracks they closed the depot at Williams and opened a new one just to the east of town known as Williams Junction. From 1961 to 1968 all passenger traffic to the Canyon departed from and returned to Williams Junction. In 1969 the Santa Fe closed this station also and demolished it after discontinuation of passenger service to the Grand Canyon. Station Agent Glenn Irvin had the unpleasant duty of closing both the Williams and Williams Junction depots.

1.3-4.5   KAIBAB NATIONAL FOREST. Just north of the overpass the train enters a beautiful stand of Ponderosa pine. As the engine barks up the grade the riders get a chance to view a small part of the largest stand of Ponderosas in the world. Most people have a mind's eye vision of Arizona being a land of sand and snakes and it comes as a surprise to find these beautiful giant stands of trees so prevalent. This is a section of the southern unit of the Kaibab and extends just a few miles until open rangeland is entered. The men and women of the National Forest Service keep this place in trust for us to enjoy. After the train ride return to the forest for restful camping, hiking, sightseeing, hunting, or fishing to complete your vacation.

0.0-4.2 PONDEROSA PINE FOREST. This is but a small part of the huge stand of Ponderosas ranging from the Grand Canyon south to the Mogollon Rim and across to New Mexico. Ponderosas are usually found between the elevations of 6000 to 9000 feet. Some of the mature trees seen from the train may be 300 to 400 years old and reach heights up to 125 feet. Occasionally some of these wonderful giants may reach ripe old ages of over 500 years. This tree has provided jobs for generations of loggers and continues to provide a livelihood for many people of the region. The Saginaw and Manistee Lumber Company headquartered in Williams for many years and harvested these trees for use as lumber, railroad ties, mine timbers and boxes of all shapes and sizes. In addition to providing jobs this forest is home to many species of wildlife. If luck is with the rider magnificent elk will make their appearance along with mule deer, pronghorn antelope, and the very elusive mountain lions and wild turkeys. Keep your eyes open throughout the trip and you may be rewarded with sights of owls, hawks, coyotes or even an occasional bald or golden eagle.

2.6-4.0   3% GRADE.   On the northbound trip the train drifts down the grade through the thinning forest to Cataract Creek at MP 4. But on the southbound trip the engine will begin to labor up the grade just after passing over the bridge. This 1.4 mile long grade is just as steep as the Apex grade but not nearly as long. The train slows and gives the passengers time to view the forest, look for animals and watch sunsets. Enjoy this part of the trip for it will all be slow as the train nears the station and the end of your journey back into a more leisurely time.

3.1   TRANSWESTERN NATURAL GAS PIPELINE. Installation of this pipeline began in 1960 with the first of two thirty inch welded steel seamless pipelines. Transwestern just completed the second loop line in 1989. These lines move natural gas from Texas, New Mexico, Oklahoma and Mexico to the California gas line at Needles, California and it continues from there on into Los Angeles. Three billion cubic feet of gas per year travel this route at the rate of eight million cubic feet daily under a pressure of 870 to 1050 pounds per square inch at four and one half to six miles per hour. Pipelines such as these safely transport huge volumes of gas without the hazards involved with surface transportation.

3.2   EL PASO NATURAL GAS PIPELINE. Three welded steel pipelines pass under the right-of-way at this point and transport natural gas from the Four Corners area to Topock, California. El Paso tranships the gas to Pacific Gas and Electric of Southern California. These safe and efficient subsurface lines move three billion cubic feet of gas in the summer and the volume is increased to four billion cubic feet in the winter. The company built the first twenty-four inch line in 1951, added a thirty inch loop

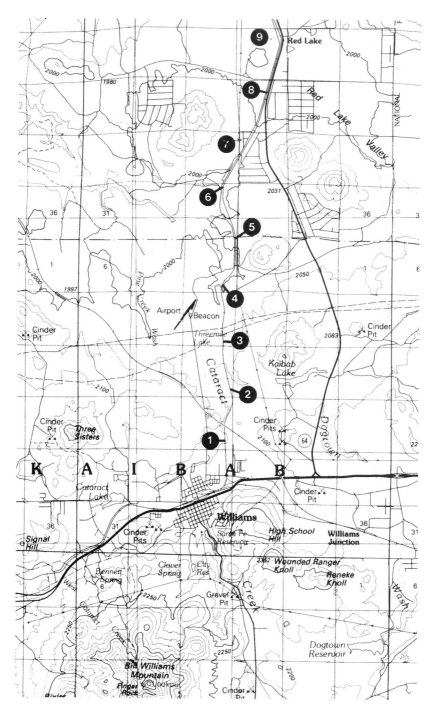

Map No. 2. Milepost 0 through 9.

line in 1953 and with increased demand added the third thirty-four inch loop line in 1956. All of this gas moves under a pressure of 850 pounds per square inch at a speed of fifteen miles per hour.

3.6   VIEW OF BILL WILLIAMS MOUNTAIN. On the northbound trip a good view of the 9,264 foot mountain south of Williams can been seen over the hills and through the trees by looking to the west toward the rear of the train and on the southbound trip by looking forward. This extinct volcano dates back four million years. Today it forms a beautiful backdrop to the City of Williams with its conifer and aspen forests. In the fall the golden aspen leaves highlight sections of the mountain. During several of the winter months snow covers the slopes which ring to the shouts of skiers enjoying the new Williams ski area. Come ride the train in the winter snows and ski Williams!

4.0   CATARACT CREEK. Just at milepost four the train rumbles out onto a 182 foot long pile and frame trestle which is the longest bridge on the line. When the train passes over the intermittent stream bed of Cataract Creek it will outrun any waters flowing down the channel to the south rim. During dry times of the year the creek is a beautiful woodland but in the spring runoff from melting snows can make this one of the more attractive sights on the trip. The monsoon season from July to September can produce thunderstorms which will make this tranquil scene turn into a raging torrent on a moment's notice. All of these waters race headlong to the north and west through Cataract Canyon, down over the rim creating the magnificent blue streams and waterfalls of Havasu Canyon, the ancestral home of the Havasupai Indians, and on into the Colorado River.

4.2-21.0 PINYON-JUNIPER WOODLAND (aka Juniper-Pinyon Woodland or P-J; pinyon is occasionally seen in Spanish as piñon). On the Kaibab Plateau P-J covers large areas at elevations roughly between 5500 and 7000 feet below the Ponderosa pine forests. At the lower elevations juniper is dominant with pinyon becoming more numerous with increasing elevation. One-seed and Utah juniper and Colorado pinyon are the most common species found in this area. Grama grasses, sagebrush and prickly pear cactus are commonly associated with the P-J woodlands along the line. A wide variety of wildlife makes the P-J home and frequently can be seen from the train. Much of the land along the line is open range and cattle of all breeds are frequently seen grazing amongst the trees.

4.5 PRONGHORN RANCH ROAD. An excellent location for photographs of the train and easily accessible from State Route 64 or Williams. From the depot in Williams go north on Grand Canyon Boulevard, turn right at the stop sign and follow the signs to the airport. At the airport entrance turn right onto the well maintained dirt road and follow it to the crossing. On Highway 64 Pronghorn Ranch Road is marked both north- and south-bound at milepost 189.6. Turn west onto the well maintained dirt road until you come to the crossing.

5.0 WILLIAMS CITY LIMIT. Northern border of the city. Reconstruction of the track and roadbed began at this location on 29 March 1989 by the new Grand Canyon Railway.

5.4 CINDER PIT. To the east two large cinder cones can be seen on the horizon and the one on the left with a large scar on its south flank is the pit. In 1906 the Santa Fe got the Arizona Supreme Court to

36

condemn this property in their favor for the purpose of mining it for volcanic cinders to be used as ballast during the rebuilding of the line. The AT&SF constructed a spur to the pit and began hauling cinders for use along the line. In the early years Chinese and Japanese laborers loaded the ballast into gondola cars with hand shovels and unloaded them in the same manner. Later the railroad installed an oil fired steam shovel in the pit to handle the loading and ballast cars with dump gates on the bottom distributed the cinders along the line where needed. Santa Fe abandoned use of the pit about 1924 and currently leases it to the State of Arizona for use on the highways.

5.9   PITT SECTION. Both the Pitt station and section are referred to on all extant plans as being located at milepost 6.5 but due to relocation of the section during rebuilding in 1905 the section remains are seen here on the east side. A former location of a section house, standard Santa Fe concrete 21' X 114' ten room bunkhouse and gang. Prior to 1906 company records referred to the section as MP 6.5. Origin of the name "Pitt" is unknown but it is probably a corruption of Cinder Pit as the name came into use at the same time the Santa Fe acquired and opened the pit. The railroad abandoned the section on 1 April 1947 but remains of the concrete bunkhouse can still be seen overgrown with junipers. The Santa Fe bulldozed it and the others along the line to save on property taxes.

6.5   PITT STATION. Actual former station location with the siding off to the east side. Once the location of a thirty-six car siding (based on 85 foot Pullman car with allowance for a four unit diesel and heater unit) and a telephone. Originally built as a spur in 1899 the railroad upgraded it to a passing track (siding) in 1905. It served as such until retirement in 1942.

7.0   **CINDER PIT WYE.** Built in 1906 to service the cinder pit to the east of the highway. Just to the north of this milepost the abandoned roadbed for the south leg of the wye to the cinder pit curves into the brush to the east. At MP 7.1 the roadbed for the north leg is more visible. The high desert environment heals slowly and takes a long time to reclaim changes caused by construction. For nearly seventy years these roadbeds have been unused yet they have not completely returned to a natural state where their location cannot be determined. This gradual process allowed the railroad historian to determine locations of several structures and tracks whose plans no longer exist. Retired about 1924.

8.3   **ESPEE ROAD.** Former location of ballast loading operations for the Grand Canyon Railway during the 1989 track renovation. During this reconstruction and on into 1990, the company trucked cinders from the pit on the reverse slope of the cone to the west of the tracks and loaded them into ballast cars with a front-end loader. Good photo location and easily accessible as it is adjacent to state highway 64 at MP 193.9.

9.0   **RED LAKE STATION.** The previous location of a telephone and a 31 car siding primarily used for cattle and sheep loading. Named for a lake across the highway to the east which takes on reddish hues from Moenkopi silt washed in during rains. The community boasted a post office for a short time in 1888 and a telegraph office operated for a short period in the early 1900s. Originally built as a spur in 1899 crews extended and upgraded it to a siding in 1905 and to its present size in 1928. Probably abandoned in 1956 with tracks retired in 1974.

13.7 POWER TRANSMISSION LINES. Certainly not esthetically pleasing but these Arizona Public Service lines provide necessary electrical power to the West Wing switch yard in Phoenix, Arizona from the Navajo Generating Station at Page, Arizona. During peak output 500,000 volts of electricity traverse these lines to supply homes and businesses in central Arizona.

14.8 BLY STATION—BEALE ROAD. Formerly the location of a nine car spur and a telephone. Built for Fletcher D. Bly by the Santa Fe in 1917. The contract included a concrete water tank and corrals for sheep loading. Retired by the railroad on 12 December 1941 they used the material from the spur for construction of the spur at MP 18. The trail seen disappearing into the scrub up the hill to the west at this point is the remains of the Beale Road. Someone standing here in September 1857 would have been treated to a sight which would have been equal to many circuses of the day. Lt. Edward F. Beale crossed here with a caravan of camels and their Turkish and Greek handlers dressed in native clothing. The Army commissioned this naval lieutenant to test the feasibility of camels for service in the arid southwest. Several reasons, including the Civil War and misunderstanding of the animal's capabilities, doomed the project and descendents of these foreign four legged visitors could be seen wandering the deserts of western Arizona as late as the 1930s. Beale's road from Ft. Smith, Arkansas to California saw heavy service from 1860 to 1882. Yesterday's Route 66 and today's Interstate 40 basically follow the route Beale surveyed and carved along the 35th parallel.

16.5-18.0 RED LAKE WASH. Shortly after Bly the tracks continue to wander through the

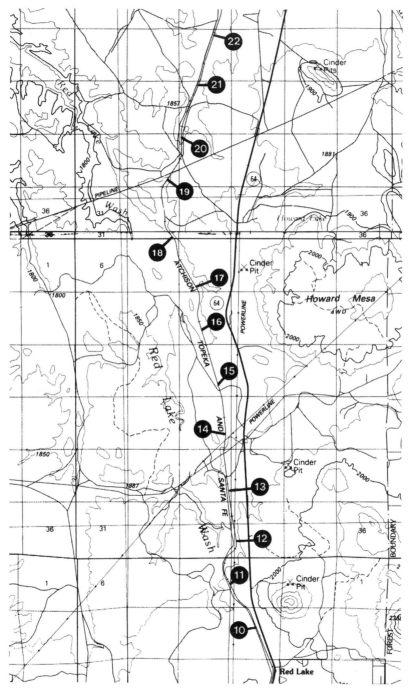

Map No. 3. Milepost 10 through 22.

40

Pinyon-Juniper woodland and then drop into a long, pretty valley extending out to the northwest. They curve and cross a bridge over Red Lake Wash. Usually dry, this drainage can become a raging red torrent during any one of this region's frequent summer thunderstorms. The curve and grades offer good views of the locomotive from the west side of the cars.

18.0   **VIEW TO WEST.** As the train climbs up out of Red Lake Wash the western view expands to the horizon. Mountains silhouetted against an azure sky occasionally spotted by puffy white cumulus clouds appear to be a few miles away and actually are more than thirty. The highest at 7439 feet is Mount Floyd. It is flanked by Round and Trinity mountains to the north. Both of these are over 7000 feet.

18.2   **MP 18 SECTION.** Previously the location of a section house, bunkhouse, gang and a telephone. After abolishment of the sections at Valle and Anita in 1941 and 1942, the section at MP 18 became responsible for maintenance of track from MP 10.0 to MP 45.0. The Williams section covered MP 0.0 to MP 10.0 and the Grand Canyon section covered MP 45.0 to 63.8. The railroad abolished this section on 15 June 1954. At this time and until abandonment of the line the sections at Williams and Grand Canyon split responsibilities for maintenance at MP 39.0. The company installed a 610 foot spur at this location in 1941 and in turn retired it in 1974. Remains of the concrete bunkhouse are easily seen to the east of the tracks.

19.2   **BLACK MESA COAL SLURRY PIPE- LINE.** Buried under the tracks and crossing from east to west is an eighteen inch welded steel pipeline used to transport coal from Black Mesa in

Arizona to the Mohave Generating Station at Laughlin, Nevada. Operated by Black Mesa Pipeline, Inc. the line carries a 50/50 slurry mixture of coal and water at a rate of five feet per second under a pressure of 650 to 700 psi. The company completed construction of this 273 mile cross country pipeline in 1970 and since that time has transferred over 72 million tons of coal in a safe and environmentally clean operation. This system runs twenty-four hours daily, three hundred and sixty-five days a year.

20.5   QUIVERO STATION. Originally built in 1899 and named Prado, or "meadow" in Spanish. This pretty meadow once served as the location of a 23 car siding and a telephone. Renamed Quivero in August of 1908 because there is a larger Prado station near Corona, California. Supposedly named for Quivera, one of the mythical cities of Cibola Coronado searched for in 1540. The reasons for choosing this name or the change of the ending from "a" to "o" are unknown. Originally built as a spur, the Santa Fe rebuilt it as a siding in 1905 and extended it in 1929 and again in 1931 to its present 23 car size. Retirement of siding tracks and turnouts came in 1974. Santa Fe built the loading pens about 1917, rebuilt them in 1936 and in 1974 retired and sold them in place. Local cattle and sheep ranches still use them. The Grand Canyon Railway rebuilt the spur in 1992 as a passing track for maintenance of way equipment.

22.2   LARGE CATTLE TANK. Water is a precious commodity in this region and cattle operations must use every means at their disposal to trap whatever rainfall is available. Ranchers bulldoze catchments on drainages to catch the runoff from rain and snow melt that would otherwise be lost. This large tank belongs to the Triple E Livestock & Land Company and is referred to as Mud Tank. Usually this tank has several cross breed cattle around it and occasionally some pronghorns (antelope) can be seen here because a good sized herd frequents the area.

26.7   NORTH RIM. When the northbound train tops a grade and curves to the left at this point a great view of the north rim of the Grand Canyon over the hills and plains of the Kaibab Plateau opens up on the east side. The rim is about fifty miles away and the early morning light reflects the colors very well. Due to the steadily rising terrain of the Kaibab Plateau the north rim is one thousand feet higher than the south rim and because of this it appears as a cliff on the horizon.

26.7   RED BUTTE. At the same point riders have a good view to the northeast of Red Butte standing about 1300 feet above the surrounding terrain. Even at a distance of fifteen miles a good perspective can be realized as to what this area looked like 200 million years ago. The red layer is composed of Moenkopi sandstone and mudstones which had been deposited in a tidal flat environment over this entire region. Due to the uplifting of the Kaibab Plateau this formation underwent severe fracturing and opened itself up to rapid erosion. Today all of the Moenkopi is gone from the plateau except for Red Butte. At the extreme top, a thick layer of basaltic lava continues to protect this last remnant outcrop.

28.5-36.7 SAN FRANCISCO PEAKS. While the train curves across the open plains and rises and falls with the rolling hills good views of the magnificent San Francisco Peaks appear to the east. This dormant volcano is about thirty miles to the east and sports a snow cap much of the year. Calculated to have

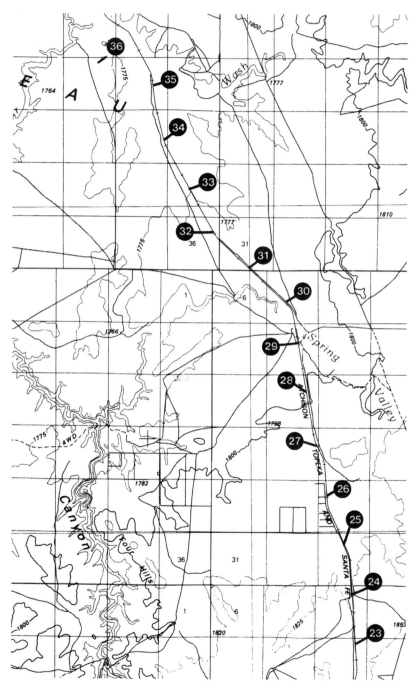

Map No. 4. Milepost 23 through 36.

been over fifteen thousand feet high before it blew its top much like Mt. St. Helens, it now has several peaks around the collapsed caldera. Mt. Humphrys is the highest at 12,633 feet and one of its companions, Mt. Agassiz, stands at 12,356 feet. These two are the highest peaks in Arizona.

29.0   VALLE STATION. Former location of a section house, bunkhouse, gang, telephone and a 37 car siding for cattle and sheep loading. Originally built as a spur in 1899 the Santa Fe rebuilt it as a siding in 1905 and extended it in March, 1929 to its present size. Named in Spanish for Spring Valley. The railroad built the loading chutes for the Grand Canyon Sheep Company in 1919. It is presently the headquarters of the Bar Heart Ranch. The owners purchased all of the cattle loading facilities in 1941 when the railroad retired them in place. Although this ranch has supported both cattle and sheep it apparently has not always been so exclusive for one still hears of the story of a bull elk who moved into the pens and made himself to home. He stayed for several days until the Game and Fish Department came out to relocate him. Cattle are still loaded from this location today but all transportation is handled by truck. This station occasionally appears in the record as Abra Crossing. Abra ceased to be used in the 1930s and is probably an Anglo corruption of cabra, the Spanish word for sheep. The Santa Fe abolished the section on 19 January 1941 and retired the siding track and turnouts in 1974. Remains of the concrete section gang bunkhouse are easily seen to the west of the tracks inside the fence line. During the 1950s, the railroad bulldozed many of the unused structures along the line to save on taxes.

29.1   SPRING VALLEY WASH. At the north end of the Bar Heart Ranch the train pulls

out onto a concrete bridge and fill arrangement span-
ning Spring Valley Wash. In the early years of the line
this wash had been crossed by the line's longest pile and
frame trestle. It exceeded three hundred feet in length
and fifty feet in height. Apparently the Santa Fe
engineers believed the system now in use to be easier
and cheaper to maintain and therefore replaced the
wooden bridge. On the east side of the train riders are
afforded a good look at folded Kaibab limestone at the
top of the north bank of the wash. When this plateau
underwent tectonic uplifting much of the horizontal
strata in the region yielded to the great pressures and
folded as seen here.

33.5   **SAN FRANCISCO PEAKS AND RED
BUTTE.** Another good view of both are seen
off to the east.

34.8-36.0 MILLER WASH.   Here the train passes
onto a section of track crossing Miller Wash
several times. Four bridges span this intermittent
stream in little more than a mile. Prior to 1916 the
roadbed followed the wash instead of cutting through
the limestone hills. The old right-of-way can still be
seen from both sides of the train winding along with the
stream bed. An accident in 1916 resulted in the
straightening of the line and removal of one half mile of
curving track. In years gone by a female mountain lion
waited for the daily train in order to be fed by the crew
members at MP 35. Look closely and maybe you will see
her children's children come to resume the vigil.

36.0   **1916 WRECK.** On the night of 29 July 1916
engineer "Dutch" Oswald entered upon the
bridge from the north. He held the train to minimum
speed because the entire northland had been subjected
to heavy thunderstorms all day long and he wanted to

be sure of the track. He couldn't know or see that a huge storm had dumped thousands of tons of hail that blocked up the four bridges and diverted flood waters over the abutments, washing them out. The locomotive settled down into the wash and the fireman, Fred Terry, became trapped between the engine and tender. A steam pipe burst and severely scalded the unfortunate Terry. Due to the slow speed no passengers had been hurt but Oswald lost some toes to frostbite caused by standing in the hail for hours and tending to Terry. Before help could be summoned, the hapless fireman succumbed to his injuries.

37.3   POWER TRANSMISSSION LINES.
These Arizona Public Service power lines originate at the Four Corners Generating Station and cross all of Arizona to the El Dorado switching station between Boulder City and Searchlight, Nevada. Here the 500,000 volts carried during peak output enters the western power grid for distribution to homes and businesses.

37.7   WILLAHA STATION. A former location of
a section bunkhouse, telephone and a 24 car siding for cattle, sheep and ore loading. Named after a Supai Indian word meaning "watering place." Originally built as a spur in 1899 the Santa Fe extended and upgraded it to a siding in 1905. The railroad built the water cistern, warehouse and corrals for the C. L. DeRyder ranch in 1919 and renovated them in 1940. Leases extended to the Azurite Copper Company in 1903 and the Houge Mining Company in 1907 provided for copper ore loading. The date of section abolishment is unknown but the Santa Fe retired the siding track and turnouts in 1974. A seven mile long well maintained dirt road leads to this location from state highway 64. Turn west from the highway at MP 221.4.

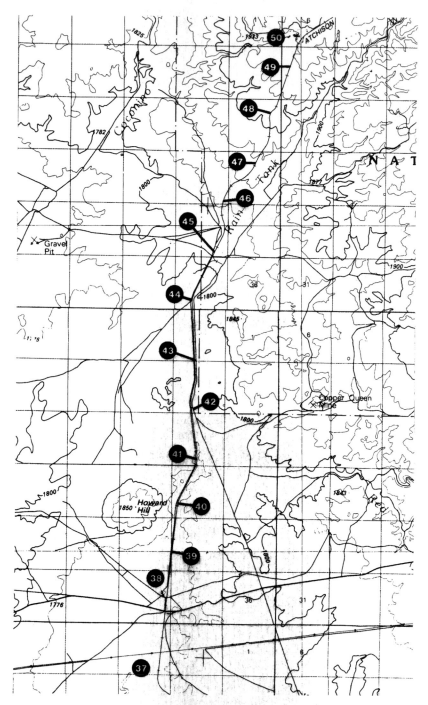

Map No. 5. Milepost 37 through 50.

However, it is not advisable to use this road in wet weather. The Grand Canyon Railway rebuilt the siding in 1990 for use as a passing track for trains and maintenance of way equipment. Ballast loading operations are also conducted.

38.1　　**CATTLE TANK.**　Just to the north of the Willaha crossing the train crosses over a bridge and large cattle tank. Usually the tank on the west side holds water much of the year but in wet years the entire tank on both sides of the track is filled and forms a large lake. This is Railroad Tank on the Willaha Ranch and several different breeds of cattle are frequently seen here with the larger hump-backed Brahmas being the most unusual.

40.7　　**PHONE LINE ENDS.**　At one time the telegraph and telephone line from Williams to the Grand Canyon ran the entire length on the west side of the tracks. Today it extends only to this point where it takes off to the west to service a ranch some ten miles out.

42.1　　**COPPER QUEEN CLAIMS.**　Mining of copper at these claims in the hills to the east started in 1901 along with the Anita mines. The same people who mined the vast copper pits in Jerome worked these breccia pipes for the very rich ore produced here. Although the ore assayed very high the mines did not contain a sufficient amount to make them profitable and they failed.

43.8　　**WOODIN STATION.**　Originally the location of a one car spur for cattle and sheep loading and upgraded to three car capacity on 15 December 1937. Built by the Santa Fe in 1917 for the Pittman Valley Land and Cattle Company and later leased to the Grand Canyon Sheep Company in 1930 and again in 1937 to the Babbitt Brothers Trading Company. Unknown as to the origin of the name but in all probability the Santa Fe named it after W. H. Woodin, president of the American Car and Foundry Company, which built railroad cars. The railway retired the spur track and turnout in 1974.

44.4-59.9 KAIBAB NATIONAL FOREST. At this point the tracks again cross into the Kaibab forest. Here the train is on the plains of Anita but just north of the road crossing Pinyon-Juniper growth begins and blends into the Ponderosa pine of this northern forest unit. From this point on until the National Park is entered the train will travel through public lands maintained for us by the people of the Forest Service. Keep your eyes open for the many species of wildlife that live and thrive in this area.

44.9 ANITA STATION. The original destination of the railroad for the purpose of servicing company mining interests Anita is the former location of a section house, bunkhouse, gang, telephone, stock yards, Forest Service headquarters, school, post office, 40 car wye, 12 car water track, ore loading ramp, the 2.87 mile spur to the Anita Mines, a 1,250 foot siding (later shortened in September, 1917 to a four car spur for the Forest Service), two water tanks and a fair sized community. Named for Anita Lombard and originally called Anita Junction when built in 1899. William Lockridge contracted with the Santa Fe for construction of the ore ramp in 1918. On 31 January 1942 the company abolished the section and by 1956 all structures except for the stock yard and ore ramp had been removed. In 1942 the railroad retired the spur track and in 1972 the water siding and wye. Remains of the station and concrete bunkhouse are easily seen to the west of the tracks just north of the crossing. A well maintained dirt road leads six miles from Highway 64 to this station. However, it is not advisable to take this road in wet weather. Turn west from the highway onto Forest Service road 347 at MP 228.

45.0 **SPUR TO ANITA MINES.** The Santa Fe & Grand Canyon Railroad began construction of the line in 1898 for the primary purpose of servicing the mines in the Anita vicinity. They built a 2.78 mile long spur from this point northeast into the hills where the claims are located. At the end of track the Anita Copper Company loaded copper ore into cars from a tipple. Ruins of this tipple and mines can still be seen today.

45.4 **CO BAR CORRAL.** Built in 1909 by the Santa Fe for the CO Bar Cattle Company (Babbitt Brothers) and enlarged in 1913. The railroad retired the yards in place in 1974 and sold them to the CO Bar. They are still used to load cattle on trucks for shipment to market.

45.6-51.9 PINION-JUNIPER WOODLAND. This area is very similar to the P-J woodland already described at MP 4.2. However the density of growth is greater and the slope steeper here. Wildlife abounds so keep your eyes open but don't be too surprised to see cattle wandering amongst the trees as ranchers lease this land for grazing.

45.7-52.0 APEX GRADE. The grade starts out on an easy slope and curves up the steeper Kaibab limestone outcrops. To the east tree covered ledges are home to the Anita mines whose rich ores attracted this railroad to the region. At 3%, several grades in this section make the engine labor and the rider is treated to the sights and sounds of a steam engine barkin' in full cutoff as it twists and turns up the slope. This is the longest, continuous grade on the line and Apex station got the name from its location at the top of the longest ruling grade on the line.

47.0-48.3 VIEWS TO SOUTH AND EAST. Although the view is good on the northbound trip the rider can look out over these vast expanses more easily on the return run. As the train drifts through the curves great views of the forested slopes and plains are highlighted by the afternoon sun when it is low in the western sky. But the real treat is the array of mountains lining the southern horizon in their varying shades of blue.

50.0 HOPI STATION. A previous location of a 23 car siding and telephone. The Santa Fe most likely established this siding as a doubling track for the five mile long Anita-Apex grade. They later used it as a set out for the logging trains from Apex. It is named after the Hopi Indians. Established about 1901 as a spur they later extended it in 1905 and again in 1928 as a siding. The railroad retired the siding on 14 November 1942 with the removal of rails, switches and switch ties.

51.9-63.8 PONDEROSA PINE. As at the southern end of the line the Ponderosa pine forests here are equally as magnificent. The trees appear thicker in the northern unit of the Kaibab and the Park but in reality the difference comes from the increased undergrowth and the introduction of scrub oaks.

52.0 IMBLEAU (formerly APEX) STATION. The former location of a section house, bunkhouse, gang, telephone and a 31 car siding. Originally built as a passing track in 1901 at the top of the Anita-Apex grade. Renamed by the GCR in 2001 to honor Roadmaster Sam Imbleau who had been instrumental in upgrade and maintenance of the right of way from the rebuilding in 1989. In 1928 it became the center for the Saginaw and Manister Lumber Company logging operations in the Anita-Moqui district of the Kaibab National Forest. They contracted with the Santa Fe for the building of an 85 car wye and spur which the Saginaw extended twenty six miles to the east. The Santa Fe also built them an additional 27 car siding in 1930. Apex has been referred to as the high point on the line but in actuality Grand Canyon station is higher. The name originated from the fact that Apex is at the top of the longest 3% grade on the line. On 1 June 1930 the Santa Fe abolished the section and in 1942 retired the wye and interchange track with removal of rails, switches and ties. The siding remained in service until retired in 1954. Remains of the concrete bunkhouse are still standing and easily seen to the west of the tracks. Present location of a spur track built by the Grand Canyon Railway in 1992 as a maintenance of way passing track. An environmental impact study finished in 1993 cleared the way for planned extension to the Grand Canyon Airport. This service will work in conjunction with the the National Park Service General Management Plan to provide alternative transportation into the National Park for airline passengers and highway travelers in order to reduce traffic congestion and pollution within the Park.

54.0-58.0 COCONINO CANYON. Here the rider is treated to a variety of sights and sounds. The canyon follows Coconino Wash, cut down over the millenia through layers of Kaibab limestone and into the Toroweap Formation. Because of the curves and grade the train slows down and drifts into the canyon.

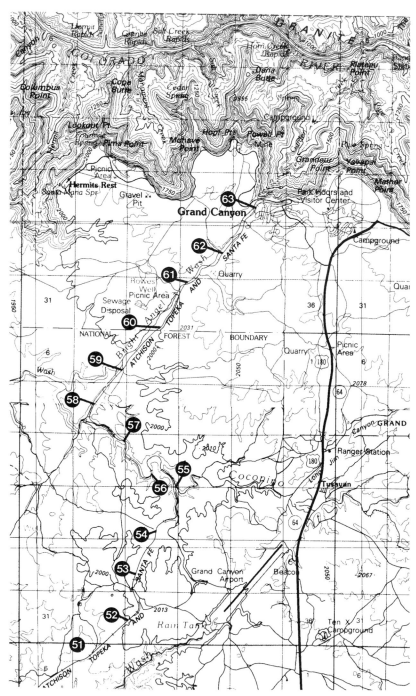

Map No. 6. Milepost 51 through Grand Canyon.

Trees and brush lining the walls and floor of the wash help to make this a pleasant and relaxing part of the trip. Several bridges are crossed and the twists and turns of the canyon make for great views of the locomotive from either side of the cars. After passing Coconino station the grade increases for the run up to the south rim of the Grand Canyon. On the southbound trip the engine works up the long grade and due to the close confines of the canyon the exhaust of the engine echoes all around the train, providing the rider a unique and pleasurable experience.

55.0-56.0 SWITCHBACKS. An interesting situation occurs in this mile of track. The right-of-way follows the bed of the wash and the meander of the stream doubles back on itself. Keep track of the sun and it will be noted at one point to be on one side of the train and in a short distance on the other side and then return to the original side. Because of the depth of the canyon the only way to keep track of the two 180° changes of direction the train makes here is by watching the sun's position.

57.2 COCONINO STATION. Once the location of a 34 car siding built in 1900 as a passing track and a telephone. In 1916 a rancher named Henderson contracted with the railroad for construction of a concrete box water tank for his cattle still seen to the east of the track down the slope. This station served temporarily as the northern terminus of the line and transfer point for the Grand Canyon stage while construction by the SF&GCRR and later the AT&SFRy moved north to the rim. The railroad used this siding at least part of the time to set out water cars from the Grand Canyon. Its name comes from the wash in which it is located. Retirement of the siding probably occurred in 1954.

58.9   **HILLTOP CROSSING.** In the early days of the railroad Bill Bass had arranged with the Santa Fe for a flag stop here to collect his customers for the trip by coach to his camp at Havasupai Point. The conductor scheduled a stop to detrain passengers on the northbound trains. If Bass had returning passengers he simply flagged the southbound and put them on board for the trip to Williams. Good photo location and access to Coconino Canyon. It is suggested you have the Kaibab Forest map available from the Forest Service while driving in this area. A six mile long well maintained dirt road leads to this location from milepost 236 on state highway 64 from the south end of Moqui Lodge. This is Forest Service road 605 and definitely not recommended for travel in wet weather.

59.2   **HIGHLAND MARY.** In 1916 Sanford Rowe patented this land as the Highland Mary claim along with the Highland Mary mill site further up the line at what is now known as Rowe's Well. Tom (a Santa Fe engineer) and Mattie Gordon purchased the land in 1937 and built the home of native rock and wood. Over the years the property passed through several hands. From 1958 to 1969 the Western Gold & Uranium Company used the property for quarters to house employees of the Orphan Mine on the south rim of the Canyon in the National Park. The company sold the house and property to the present owners in 1978. Erik, Sue, and Fabienne Gueissaz come out to wave at the train whenever they are home.

59.9   **NATIONAL PARK BOUNDARY AND GRAND CANYON YARD LIMIT.** At this point the train passes into the Grand Canyon National Park and moves cautiously at restricted speeds. A fence line extending east and west denotes the boundary line. The right-of-way follows Bright Angel Wash for the remainder of the trip. Good photo locations all along this stretch are easily accessible on a good dirt road generally referred to as Rowe's Well Road, from hilltop crossing or Grand Canyon Village. Again, these roads are not recommended for travel in wet weather.

60.7 ROWE'S WELL. Sanford Rowe bought out the Williams livery business of William W. "Billy" Bass in 1892 and spent the next several years supplying the south rim business people with their freight requirements. He staked some mineral claims about three miles west and south of the village and built a small log hotel there. Over the years it grew into a tourist complex with a hotel, cabins and an entertainment facility which included a bowling alley and dance floor. A popular spot with the residents of the village the "watering hole" provided some relief from the ever-present tourists. Here, they could get away and have a friendly drink, bowl a few lines and do some dancing. By the late 1950s many of the wooden frame and log buildings had deteriorated to a condition beyond repair and demolition by the Park Service became necessary to ensure safety and the esthetics of the natural scene. In April of 1961 the Park removed the last structures and all that remains today of Rowe's Well is a picnic ramada next to the tracks.

62.6 WATER TREATMENT PLANT. Built in 1972 to replace the original 1926 plant built by the Santa Fe. This is a modern and efficient facility but the filters of the old plant are still in use. The National Park Service preserves it as a historic engineering work to showcase pioneer treatment of sewage and reuse of effluent under semi-arid conditions.

63.3 BRIGHT ANGEL FAULT. As the train moves slowly up the grade it begins a turn to the right and comes to a crossing. At this point the Grand Canyon itself is visible on the north side of the train. The Bright Angel Fault traverses the entire canyon and created this viewpoint. From Coconino Canyon the train has been following this fault up Bright Angel Wash.

62.9   GRAND CANYON YARDS. From this point the train moves into the yards and up past the historic Bright Angel Lodge and powerhouse to the depot. After the passengers are discharged, the crew backs the train onto the wye (with a grade of 3.7%), completes the turning movements, and backs into the station. They uncouple the locomotive and return to the tail of the wye where it is serviced for the trip to Williams. When servicing is complete the engine rejoins the train at the station.

63.7   GRAND CANYON STATION. Welcome to the Grand Canyon. Passengers arrive today much as did those who rode the first train from Williams to the Grand Canyon on 17 September 1901. The primary difference is that today's passengers arrive at a newer station in the historic district of the Grand Canyon National Park. Virtually all of the buildings around the yards were built by the Santa Fe Railway over a period of fifty-five years. Most are listed on the National Register of Historic Places. To see the Canyon walk toward the 1910 vintage depot and cross the road to the walkway up the hill to the north. This path passes right by the front door of the magnificent El Tovar Hotel. In continuous operation since January, 1905, you might wish to dine at its splendid restaurant. A fine meal can also be found at the 1935 Bright Angel Lodge. Or just take the time to relax and enjoy the view.
During the years of operation this station served as the northern terminus of the railway with

passenger and freight station facilities, telegraph, several tracks used as set outs for trains, a wye for reversing train direction, water tracks for off-loading water into cisterns and tanks, and a section gang. Tracks are numbered from 1 to 41 yet the Canyon yards never had 41 tracks at any one time. To complicate matters the Santa Fe relocated, renumbered or combined several tracks over the years. To confuse the issue even more, tracks had assigned names related to their function such as, old flume, garbage, oil, gasoline, barn, engine, engine storage, house and power house spur. In 1950 engineering drawings set the car capacity for the yards at 226 with the stem of the wye able to hold a sixteen car passenger train with a four unit passenger/freight diesel and heater unit. On 16 May 1969 the Santa Fe terminated all services and closed the station. The section house and bunkhouse had been located along the east side of the wye. Abolishment of the section came on 26 May 1969 and from this time on the Williams section handled all maintenance on the line. Between 13 and 20 June 1974 the last retirements of track occurred with removal of tracks 3, 4, 17, 21, 23, 27, 29, 33, 35 and 37.

Albeit within the National Park, the Grand Canyon Railway maintains the yards, depot and crossings just as did the Santa Fe before them. When ridership increases other tracks in the yards will be overhauled and placed back into service. In anticipation for service from the airport, the railroad has upgraded the tracks at the new Park Service Maswik depot and transportation center.

Although the yards will never again be filled to capacity with cars brought in by Shriner, Boy Scouts and American Legion specials, they are again alive with the sights and sounds of steam trains and happy passengers visiting one of the greatest places on earth.

GCRy's 1915 vintage Jordan Spreader in new yellow and black livery stands ready to clear the line of snow whenever it exceeds the capacity of the steam and diesel engines.

Track crewmen celebrate the arrival at the Cañon of the first scheduled Williams to Grand Canyon train on 11 September 1989. This ballast train is the first to arrive at the depot since June, 1974.

Track gang uses a front-end loader to set rail into place after laying the ties and spiking the tie plates. Rails are then gaged, spiked down and aligned. Ballast is added and a surfacing machine then levels, precision aligns and finishes the surface to first class condition.

Bridge and building gang drilling bolt holes after setting a new bridge beam in place near MP 13.

Track gang works with a tie machine and tamper near MP 62.

Ballast train waits to be loaded at Espee Road and Highway 64.

Track crews turn into loggers. Tree removal operations in the Grand Canyon yards.

PLANTS AND TREES

As described in the section on the Grand Canyon Region, Arizona biospheres are divided into life zones. These zones dictate the plant communities that survive or flourish within their boundaries. Keep in mind these boundaries are general in scope because they vary according to slope exposure. A northerly slope has vegetation from higher elevations while a southerly slope hosts species generally considered to be indigenous to zones of lower elevation.

Five of the seven defined life zones can be found between the Colorado River at the bottom of the Grand Canyon and Williams. This section will try to outline several of the more common and easily recognized plant species and will not try to encompass all known varieties. For the individual who desires a thorough study of the plants and animals of the region there are several outstanding texts available for this purpose.

The Colorado River at the bottom of the Canyon combines two ecosystems. One is the plant community belonging to the Lower Sonoran desert life zone and the other is the riparian habitat. Riparian plants are indigenous to the banks of rivers and streams and are unique in themselves.

Riparian Habitat-Lower Sonoran Zone

Tamarisk, *Tamarix pentrandra*, is the dominant plant along the Colorado River. Commonly referred to as Salt-cedar it is an introduced species and thrives with the year-round supply of water. It flowers from March to August in great clusters.

Fremont Cottonwood, *Populus fremontii* can be found along tributary streams of the Colorado in the side canyons. With large and spreading branches this beautiful giant can reach over fifty feet and provides welcome shade to the inner canyon traveler. Several can be seen from the south rim when the visitor looks down at Indian Gardens.

Desert-willow, *Chilopsis linearis* is generally found along the river as a shrub and occasionally as a tree up to thirty feet. Between April and August it sports small, beautiful bell-shaped flowers and pod-like fruit.

Seep-willow, *Baccharis glutinosa* is a thicket forming shrub growing to ten feet or more. Of the sunflower family it hardly resembles its cousin when it blooms. Found along the river.

Arroyo Willow, *Salix lasiolepis* found along the river or in moist seeps as a shrub. One of several willows found in the Canyon it is a typical, but not the most common species.

Netleaf Hackberry, *Celtis reticulata* usually located near the river as a shrub it has small clustered or solitary flowers.

Arizona Walnut, *Juglans major* found only in Havasu Canyon this tree grows to over fifty feet. It produces flowers in male and female varieties and a one inch diameter nut.

Plants associated more closely with the Lower Sonoran zone have no association with riparian habitats. These are found away from the river but occasionally can be seen in close proximity.

Creosote bush, *Larrea tridentata* is a strong smelling shrub found in washes, alluvial fans and canyons. It produces beautiful yellow flowers between February and April.

Four-winged Saltbush, *Atriplex canescens* is a low lying scrub brush with greenish white leaves. Mostly found in saline soil it produces very small white flowers.

Utah Agave, *Agave utahensis* is more commonly called the Century Plant. It produces long, fleshy leaves with sharp points. Its most beautiful feature occurs sometime between May to July and at the age of fifteen to twenty-five years when it sends a stalk of flowers up to fifteen feet in height. Enjoy this while you can for the plant then dies.

Blackbrush, *Coleogyne ramosissima* is a shrub of the rose family reaching heights of six feet. Branches end in spines so handle this plant as any other rose. Flowers appear from March to May and are usually yellow and very small.

Mesquite, *Prosopsis juliflora* occurs as a shrub or small tree up to twenty feet in height in washes and alluvial fans. Don't be too quick to reach for the beautiful, fragrant bottlebrush flowers as the tree is well equipped with thorns. These flowers and seed pods form between May and July.

Datil Yucca, *Yucca baccata* is found from the river to the Tonto platform. It produces sharply pointed, fleshy leaves with fibres at the edges. A drooping, white petaled flower rises on a stalk between April and July along with a banana-like fruit.

Catclaw, *Acacia greggii* is a relative of the mesquite and appears in much the same habitats but more likely to form thickets. Very similar in appearance to the mesquite its flowers are smaller and bloom between April and October.

Mormon Tea, *Ephedra viridis* is one of several species found in the Canyon. All are stem-like jointed plants with exceptionally small leaves. All produce small cones with the male sporting miniature flowers.

Cacti of many varieties and species are found in this zone. Species include nearly everything found in Arizona from Barrel *Ferocactus acanthodes*, Cholla *Opuntia whipplei*, Prickly Pear *Opuntia polyacantha* and Hedgehog *Echinocereus engelmannii* to name a few. All have spines and sport beautiful flowers sometime between February and June.

Upper Sonoran Zone

This zone features many of the plants already described plus several other species. In the Canyon this zone extends to the south rim. Plants indigenous to this zone are also represented in the Pinyon-Juniper Woodlands along the right-of-way.

Colorado Pinyon, *Pinus edulis* is found in a wide range of habitats from four to seven thousand feet. It grows as a very fragrant rounded tree upwards of forty-five feet with leaves (needles) in

Ballast dumping on a partly washed-out culvert. Years of neglect left the track in usable condition but in need of serious repair. Weather and tie thieves created most of the work on the line which had not seen regular maintenance for twenty-five years.

Ballast cars and track crews laying ballast on the tracks near MP 61. These cars are capable of both side-dump and bottom-dump operations. The crew at the last car is using the side-dump to fill in the shoulders of the roadbed. The car in the foreground is bottom-dumping ballast between the rails.

Although the company has a good roster of track machines some of the work is still done as it was over one hundred years ago. Driving in loose spikes requires a two man team. One man raises the tie up to the rail with a bar while the other drives the spike with a maul.

All of the national park crossings required replacement. The Santa Fe installed the ties being removed here over fifty years ago and they have since remained buried. In order to keep traffic problems to a minimum the GCRy crews replaced all six crossings in a two day period.

pairs. They produce cones with edible seeds prized by Indians and gourmets called piñon nuts.

Utah Juniper, *Juniperus osteosperma* looks like a pine tree but is actually from the cypress family. This tree can grow to twenty-five feet and pervades most of the zones from the Upper Sonoran to the Boreal. The leaves are scale-like with blue berry-like cones.

Gambel Oak, *Quercus gambelii* is found below and above the rim. Usually it forms shrubs or small trees up to thirty feet. Oaks are seen frequently in Coconino Canyon and are splendidly dressed out in red during the fall. They produce a bit elongated but typical oak leaf and acorns.

Rubber Rabbitbush, *Chrysothamnus nauseosus* is seen all along the line mostly in the P-J woodland and desert scrub communities. Another member of the sunflower family it forms a very large shrub reaching sizes of up to seven feet. A very fragrant plant it clusters small yellow flowers at the tops of the twig-like branches.

Cliff Rose, *Cowania mexicana* can be found as a shrub or small tree in several habitats from the south rim to the forests. A member of the rose family it presents a problem in deciding which is more beautiful—the flowers or fruit it produces from April to June. The flowers are small and have petals while the fruit is a small feathery plume.

Big Sagebrush, *Artemesia tridentata* is a shrub and another member of the sunflower family which doesn't look anything like its cousin. Found on the rim and along most of the right-of-way in profusion the leaves are silver and very fragrant. Small yellow flowers bloom with the wet seasons.

Broom Snakeweed, *Gutierrezia sarothrae* can be found in dry open locations under and on the rim and in the forests. It produces numerous very small yellow flowers from July to November.

Fernbush, *Chamaebatiaria millefolium* is another rose family member found along much of the line in the forests and on the rim. This shrub produces pretty white flowers between August and September.

Apache Plume, *Fallugia paradoxa* also of the rose family the Apache Plume is a shrub found in more open environments and washes. Like the Cliff Rose it also produces a pretty flower and a purple feathery plumed fruit between April and June.

Transition Zone

Along the Grand Canyon Railway the Transition Zone provides the rider with a view of some of the more magnificent forests in the western United States. Generally termed Ponderosa pine forest it includes many of the plants already mentioned and several others graded in and out of the big trees.

Ponderosa Pine, *Pinus ponderosa* or, as it is sometimes known, Western Yellow Pine is the dominant tree of the south rim and the area around Williams. They grow to heights of up to one hundred and fifty feet and live to a ripe old age of several hundred years if undisturbed. Needles are in bundles of three and reach lengths of up to twelve inches. It produces large cones much in demand by craftspeople but squirrels appreciate the seeds as food. For an unusual treat smell closely and carefully between the ridges in the bark. You'll find a pleasant smell of either vanilla or butterscotch.

Littleleaf Mountain Mahogany, *Cercocarpus intricatus* is a shrub growing up to five feet and another member of the rose family. It grows below and on the rim and produces many miniature flowers and long feathery fruits. Beware the sharp spine-like branch tips.

True Mountain Mahogany, *Cercocarpus montanus* is very similar yet grows in excess of ten feet and produces a different type of flower.

Greenleaf Manzanita, *Arctostaphylos pungens* is found in the forests at both ends of the line. Easily recognized by its reddish stems with strips peeling off. This shrub produces white bulb shaped flowers in clusters and a berry-like fruit in May and June.

When the train moves out of the Pinyon-Juniper Woodland it crosses the high desert plains of the Coconino Plateau. These grasslands produce many different kinds of bunchgrasses to include blue and black grama, galleta, Arizona fescue, sand and spike dropseed, spike muhly and alkali sacaton. Shrubs such as chamiza are on the rebound on well tended ranches and big sage is common. Wildflowers spring up in profusion with every rainfall. Many of these are also found in the Transition Zone and all provide good graze and browse for cattle and wildlife.

The Fray Marcos hotel on 29 March 1989, the day workmen began the rehabilitation of the structure. Built in 1908 this Fred Harvey hotel and restaurant provided Williams and the Santa Fe with a first class facility. Entry to the old hotel and dining room is in the alcove to the left.

Fray Marcos' lobby entry alcove as it appeared in March. Bricks and boards covered the windows and doors but vandals forced their way in and damaged much of the building. The door straight ahead was the entrance to the restaurant and the door to the right gave access to the lobby of the hotel.

The Santa Fe field engineer's office on the day GCRy workmen began the cleanup of the building. Vandals had broken into the office and scattered documents and engineering drawings. A leaking ceiling turned much of the paper into pulp. The company historian sifted through all of this material in order to salvage the engineering history of the line.

Workmen on the roof of the Fray Marcos remove tons of cinders installed by the Santa Fe to effect a peaked roof that facilitated drainage. As long as they maintained the asphalt roofing it worked. Once it started to leak the cinders acted as a reservoir.

Boreal Zone

At either end of the line the Transition Zone grades into the Boreal Zone. Although several plants of the Canadian and Hudsonian Zones (which make up the Boreal) are found here not all of the species are represented.

Douglas Fir, *Pseudotsuga menziesii* can reach heights of ninety feet or more and is found below and above the south rim and in the forests around Williams. Single needles are spread around a stem giving them a bushy look. Cones have unusual three pronged brachts. This tree provided the basis for the original studies by its namesake who founded the science of dendrochronology or tree ring dating.

Quaking Aspen, *Populus treuloides* reminds most Easterners of birch trees because of their white bark and black marks. Found in abundance around Williams, there are a few rare stands on the south rim. Some grow to fifty feet or more and sport green leaves in the summer and brilliant golden leaves in the fall. Its name comes from the trembling of the leaves in the slightest wind.

Engelmann Spruce, *Picea engelmanii* is a beautiful symmetrical tree but only rarely found in the forests along the line. They can grow to over one hundred feet with single needles and small cones.

White Fir, *Abies concolor* are large trees usually exceeding one hundred feet. Found below and above the south rim they normally grow in the cooler shady areas along the right-of-way. These beautiful complements to the Ponderosa pine forest grow relatively long single needles and fairly large cones.

Blue Spruce, *Picea pungens* is another beautiful and rare tree in the forests along the line. They can grow to more than seventy symmetrical feet and come equipped with very sharp single needles and large cones.

As any knowledgeable biologist can attest, this list is far from complete but it is representative of some of the more common and visible plants and trees the Grand Canyon Railway rider can identify without much difficulty. Please enjoy the forests and grasslands along the right-of-way and ensure they remain pristine for the visitors who come after you by not throwing anything from the train that may harm the environment or the beauty of the scene.

Installation of a new wooden framed peaked roof and copper scuppers made the roof watertight. If it had been done this way originally, the building might not have suffered so much water damage. In order to retain the historical integrity of the structure workmen used original fixtures whenever possible. They installed the skylight in the lower right of the photo in its original position on the framework in the center. Now it continues to provide light to the interior of the building as in the original design.

Sandblasting removed eighty-one years of accumulated paint and grime.

The original layer of paint determined the color of the restored building.

The Grand Canyon Railway museum begins to take shape just a few days before the re-inaugural. Staff members of the Sharlot Hall Museum in Prescott helped the company's curator install displays in the old Fred Harvey restaurant. Note the original tiled floors and walls. At sixteen and one-half feet the tracks in the foreground could be the world's shortest short-line railroad.

The restored Fray Marcos Hotel entryway on re-inaugural day, 17 September 1989. The doors to the museum are under the balcony. Windows and light fixtures are copies of the originals. All of the brick walkways and platforms are constructed of the original Santa Fe bricks installed in 1908.

WILDLIFE

Sharpeyed riders can frequently be rewarded with sightings of a wide variety of wildlife along the Grand Canyon Railway from the magnificent stately elk to beautiful mountain lions. Also, birds of virtually every description are either residents or transients of the area.

The following list includes something from many of the different groups of animals and birds. Not included are animals virtually impossible to see due to their size or habits. Also included are the areas where they are more likely to be seen. Look and enjoy. If you see something share it with your fellow riders by calling it out. That way those who are not as sharp at spotting animals can also enjoy our natural heritage.

On the train there are no problems concerned with wildlife but once the visitor detrains at Grand Canyon there are many animals that have become accustomed to humans and will mooch a handout at every chance. Please do not feed the animals as this will increase their dependency upon people for their survival. Another risk to humans is that rodents (usually squirrels and chipmunks) can carry fleas harboring bubonic plague bacteria. A seemingly friendly coyote, skunk or fox could be a victim of rabies. Even the biggest moochers of all, the mule deer can seriously injure an individual with their antlers or sharp hooves if startled at the wrong moment. Take care of the animals and allow them to remain wild.

Carnivores

Badger, *Taxidea taxus*. Nocturnal/diurnal. Rarely seen but they are found frequently in the Pinyon-Juniper Woodlands and grasslands.

Black Bear, *Ursus americanus*. Usually nocturnal. Rarely seen but usually found in the forested areas. For many years reputable biologists considered this animal to be in serious trouble in Arizona. Recent studies have proved bears are numerous and thriving in all regions of the state but are so wary of humans they keep their distance. Classed as a carnivore they are in reality an omnivore. Simply, this means they eat anything. In desert environments they are known to eat cactus.

Bobcat, *Lynx rufus*. Nocturnal/diurnal. A medium sized cat with spotted sides and a very short tail. They are extremely elusive and usually seen crossing a road or other open place.

Coyote, *Canis latrans*. Nocturnal/diurnal. Can be seen almost anywhere at any time. If it looks like a tan dog with a bushy tail it's a coyote. They eat almost anything.

Grey Fox, *Urocyon cinereoargenteus*. Nocturnal/ diurnal. Found in all habitats this smaller version of a coyote is grey in color and also has a bushy tail. Rodents generally make up its menu.

Mountain Lion, *Felis concolor*. Nocturnal/diurnal. Without a doubt the most striking of the carnivores this beautiful cat could appear almost anywhere from a wash in the grasslands to the Ponderosa pine forests.

Striped Skunk, *Mephitis mephitis*. Usually nocturnal but frequently seen in the daytime. Like the coyote this small, smelly critter will eat almost anything and can be spotted anywhere.

Ungulates or hoofed animals

Bighorn, *Ovis canadensis*. Diurnal. Only those riders who stay over to hike the Canyon have a chance to see these magnificent animals. On the increase after removal of the wild burros from their ancestral habitats these wily sheep can be seen in various cliffs and rocky places throughout the Canyon. A large ram can sport a complete curl in its horns.

Elk, *Cervus cacadesis*. Nocturnal/diurnal. Their range is anywhere along the line but most usually are seen in the treed areas. This is the largest member of the deer family in Arizona. It had been exterminated and then reintroduced in 1913. Presently it thrives in most of the higher elevations of the state. A bull with a full set of antlers is not easily forgotten.

Construction of the engine and car shop began with the blasting and removal of tons of volcanic rock to make room for the drop pit. Steel workers frame out the floor of the pit with reinforcing rods in preparation for the pouring of thousands of yards of concrete.

A forest of reinforcing rods mark the progress of the drop pit walls. This section of the building had to be completed before the floor or the wall foundations could be poured.

Concrete workers pour, spread and smooth yards of concrete flooring for the engine and car shop. Tons of machinery and equipment necessary for the maintenance of the engines and rolling stock require an extra thick, reinforced floor.

Framework for the overhead crane became the first structural members to rise above the concrete floor.

At the end of the 1989 season No. 18 rolled into the newly completed shop for a major overhaul. The boiler, running gear and many other systems needed a lot of work. On 1 March the work had been completed and No. 18 took her position at the head of the first train of the 1990 season.

The Chief, GCRy's parlor car, and first class dome car Coconino along the Grand Canyon line near MP 3.

Mule Deer, *Odocoileus hemionus*. Nocturnal/ diurnal. Seldom seen in the grasslands it is frequently sighted in the woodlands. Usually seen in small groups but also as solitary animals. Many wander about the overlooks and village in the National Park and are easily approached for photographs.

Pronghorn, *Antilocapra americana*. Diurnal. Can be seen anywhere along the line but most frequently in open country. With their tan color they blend into the grassy background but the white tail stands out and makes them easier to spot. Usually they are found in small groups in an open area where their exceptional eyesight and speed protect them from predators. Commonly pronghorns are called antelope but they are a uniquely North American species and not an antelope in the true sense of the word.

Slow Elk, *Bovine stupidus*. Commonly called cows. Frequently seen in all habitats along the line running to and fro whenever a train is in close proximity. Seen in every size and color configuration imaginable. The 60-40 variety is the most prevalent in this region. In order to survive on this sparse rangeland they must have a mouth sixty feet wide and run at forty miles an hour in order to get enough to eat.

Rabbits

Cottontail, *Sylvilagus audubonii*. Diurnal. Usually seen in the Pinyon-Juniper woodland.

Jackrabbit, *Lepus californicus*. Diurnal. Commonly seen in the woodlands or grasslands. Their long ears make them easy to spot.

Rodents

Abert Squirrel, *Sciurus aberti*. Diurnal. These small residents of the forests are indeed a treat if seen up close. Their coloration of blue-grey back and starkly white underbelly is remarkable but their outstanding feature is the white and black tufted ears.

Cliff Chipmunk, *Eutamias dorsalis*. Diurnal. Reddish-grey color with black and lighter stripes on the back. Frequently seen on the walls at Canyon overlooks.

Golden-mantled Ground Squirrel, *Spermophilus lateralis*. Diurnal. Reddish-gold color with black and white stripes on back. Also seen at the overlooks.

Gunnison Prairie Dog, *Cynomys gunnisoni*. Diurnal. Look for volcano shaped burrows in the open grasslands. Tan colored with white bellies they can be seen scurrying about or standing erect and doing "guard duty" on the lookout for predators.

Rock Squirrel, *Spermophilus variegatus*. Diurnal. This is the most frequently seen beggar on the walls of the overlooks. Grey in color it can have a reddish color on the back.

White-tailed Antelope Ground Squirrel, *Ammospermophilus leucurus*. Diurnal. Often seen scurrying with tail erect from burrow to burrow in the open grasslands.

Birds

At the risk of alienating bird lovers this list will lump together all categories such as raptors and wading birds. Also this is only a partial list at best. The numbers and species of birds in this region are legion so only the most visible and easily identified are covered.

Bald Eagle, *Haliaeetus leucocephalus*. Usually only sighted in transit, they have been seen soaring the canyon walls. A stark white head on a large dark brown body with a large wingspan mark this beautiful national symbol.

Clark's Nutcracker, *Nucifraga columbiana*. This pretty grey, black and white bird is commonly seen at the south rim.

Golden Eagle, *Aquila chrysaetos*. Seen occasionally soaring near the canyon walls. Dark brown body and head with large wingspan.

Great Blue Heron, *Ardea herodias*. Occasionally seen in flight at the Grand Canyon or inhabiting the shallows of the Colorado River. Its large wingspan, trailing legs in flight and blue-grey plumage make this an easy bird to identify.

Jays. Three species of Jays frequent the forests of northern Arizona but the most frequently seen is the Steller's Jay, *Cyanocitta stelleri*. A black crested head, dark blue body and large size make them easy to spot. Raucous robbers, they look for edible human trash and rob other bird's nests.

Owls. Several species live in all of the habitats along the line yet rarely seen as they are almost all nocturnal. Occasionally a Great

Today, as in the past, people make up the Grand Canyon Railway. Will Ambrose, a retired Santa Fe engineer, is an engineering consultant with the line. His father had been a conductor on the line and Will followed in his footsteps as a locomotive engineer. Today, Will's son Roy, continues the tradition as a brakeman.

Passengers arriving at the Grand Canyon depot. Except for the modern vehicles and the style of clothing this could be a scene out of the past. Many generations of travelers from all walks of life arrived at this depot just as today's riders do.

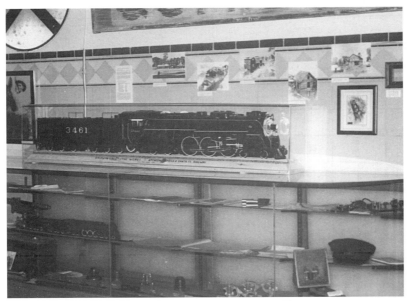

The museum is an educational and nostalic return to yesteryear through displays featuring the railroad, along with ranching, mining, and logging in the region. Artifacts, documents, photographs, and this beautiful hand built model locomotive are all housed in the historic Fray Marcos hotel.

Grand Canyon Railway passenger service attendants make the passenger's trip more enjoyable. Their primary responsibilities include seeing to the needs and comfort of the riders. Friendliness, courtesy and sharp appearance have already made them famous.

Horned Owl, *Bubo virginianus,* is startled off of its perch by the sudden appearance of the train and silently wings its way through the trees.

Peregrine Falcon, *Falco peregrinus.* Rarely seen but becoming more common below the rim. A black and white head on a dark grey body make this a strikingly beautiful bird.

Prairie Falcon, *Falco mexicanus.* Frequently seen in the open grasslands near limestone outcrops. Very light coloration makes this bird a little difficult to see but once in flight it stands out well against a blue sky.

Raven, *Corvus corax.* This black shark of the sky is all over northern Arizona and especially where people congregate. These robbers raid anywhere and tear up anything they think holds food. If human trash is not available they steal food from squirrels, or eggs and young from other birds and animals. They are commonly seen perched near trash bins or soaring on thermals.

Red-tailed Hawk, *Buteo jamaicensis.* Commonly seen along the line from woodland to grasslands either soaring or sitting on a telephone pole or fence post with good visibility. Dark brown body with a reddish tail.

Roadrunner, *Geococcyx californicus.* Seen running or gliding in either woodlands or grasslands. A very long tail, a mottled plumage and its ground hugging habits make this an easy bird to identify.

Turkey, *Meleagris gallopavo.* Well camouflaged brown plumage and a bluish red head make this a difficult bird to spot but they are commonly seen in flocks in the forests near Williams and around the National Park.

Turkey Vulture, *Cathartes aura.* Black plumage with a red head. Usually seen spiraling in the sky or perched on a tree with good visibility.

These are but a few of the many varieties of birds who make their home either temporarily or permanently on the Kaibab Plateau or in the Grand Canyon. Ardent birdwatchers can see these and everything from sparrows, flycatchers, bluebirds, orioles, wood-peckers and buntings to mockingbirds, shrikes, nighthawks and kestrals. Several species of waterfowl transit and rest in the region and even several varieties of the tiny hummingbirds come to the northlands in warmer weather.

Snakes

Most snakes found in the area are harmless but if they all look alike to the individual it is suggested a wide berth be maintained. Three species are venomous and potentially dangerous but will avoid human contact unless pressed.

Western Rattlesnake, *Crotalus viridis*. Found in the grasslands, woodlands and forests all along the line. Easily identified by dark splotches along the body, a triangular head and rattles. The Hopi Rattlesnake and Grand Canyon Rattlesnake are variations of this species.

Gopher Snake, *Pituophis melanoleucus*. Probably the most commonly seen it looks similar to and mimics a rattlesnake when agitated. It lacks the triangular head and rattles of its poisonous relative.

Kingsnakes, Whipsnakes, Garter Snakes and Long-nosed snakes are frequently seen in the region but pose no danger. All are relatively slender, fast moving and feed on insects and rodents.

Now that the rider knows what to look for it's time to enjoy what can be seen from the train and then return to the best locations for some real active bird spotting. While looking for these birds keep your eyes open for the many other varieties of animal life all around. The wildlife is there but well adapted to making it difficult to be observed. If the viewers are fortunate and rewarded for their patience by the sighting of these wonderful creatures in their native habitat they will take home irreplaceable memories. Good luck.

During the trip to the Cañon and back passenger service attendants pass out refreshments and visit with travelers. This is one of the touches that makes the GCRy a hit with passengers.

Of course there are benefits for the attendants as well. Just like in days gone by the ride to the Cañon attracts celebrities they would probably not get to meet otherwise. Such is the day when Senator Barry Goldwater rode the train. Cowboys, miners, presidents and kings.....

PEOPLE OF THE REGION

The Colorado Plateau, particularly the Grand Canyon Region, has always had a diversified population. Even in prehistoric times the native people of the area came from a variety of groups with different beliefs and cultures. Today's people with all of their modern conveniences have changed very little in this respect.

Anasazi is the name given by the Navajos to the "enemy ancestors" who inhabited the region long before recorded history. When the Navajo entered this area in the 1500s they came upon these long abandoned structures and considered them as belonging to the ancestors of the Pueblos, who they fought off and on for the last four centuries. Anthropologists have used the terms "Basketmaker" and "Pueblo" to describe these ancient peoples but now they generally use the single term Anasazi for those groups who occupied this region for over 2200 years.

Their unexplained absence from long established dwellings built and occupied between the years 1000 to 1300 AD has confounded anthropologists and archaeologists for years. Although it is known movements southward began as early as 1000, no definitive reason for the departure of such a well developed culture can be pinpointed. Scholars sift through the meager evidence in order to determine the lifestyle of these ancient people and the reasons for the abandonment of these well established communities. No one can definitely state how the Anasazi came to live here, why they departed or where they went. There are many theories ranging from drought, pestilence and depletion of resources to being overrun by enemies. All of which have merit in their own right, but we may probably never know the answers to these questions for certain.

Ancient dwellings built in the shelter of canyon walls are the trademark of the Anasazi people. Their structures are complex and built with the intelligence needed to design and complete multi-storied buildings made of rudimentary materials that have survived for more than eight hundred years. Many dwellings built today could not be expected to stand up to this record. There are many examples of the handiwork of the Anasazi in the Grand Canyon and on the Colorado Plateau. Take the time to explore some in the several national monuments and parks established for their protection.

The Spanish conquistadores arrived hard on the heels of the Navajo in 1540. These initial explorations centered in the southern and southeast corner of the Colorado Plateau in the Zuni and Hopi pueblo areas while looking for the Seven Cities of Cibola. Although Cardeñas reached the south rim of the Cañon in that year Spanish influence did not really take hold on the Plateau until the 1700s.

Spanish Franciscan missionaries began to make their appearance in the pueblos in order to bring the word of God to the "heathen" Indians. They met with varying degrees of success and failure over the centuries and made their best contribution to the understanding of this great region in 1776 when the Dominguez-

Arizona Governor Rose Mofford found the train an excellent way to enjoy the day. She rode the re-inaugural train in September and came back at Christmas with her staff for an outing. As always, the media sought her out, even on her day off.

Escalante expedition left Santa Fe on a mission of exploration. They knew of the great river and hoped it would lead to the ocean. Their trip covered a great expanse of territory in New Mexico, Arizona and Utah but did not find a way to the sea.

The plateau region remained a difficult barrier to the explorations and uses of Europeans and remained in the firm control of the many Indian tribes who inhabited the canyons, valleys and mesas. Before the Indian Wars tribes settled or wandered wherever their livelihoods took them. If the tribe existed as farmers they inhabited the best locations for growing their particular crops. These usually took the form of semi permanent villages in valleys or wash areas with a reasonable amount of water. Hunters and gatherers moved with the animals or plant sources and established temporary camps. Other nomads followed their flocks of sheep and lived where they could find the best sources of feed. Some tribes lived off of the more peaceful peoples by raiding and stealing what they needed to survive. All took from the land and returned very little to it.

Today there are fourteen recognized Indian reservations on the Colorado Plateau. The greatest number and largest are in the area adjacent to the Grand Canyon. Havasupai, Hopi, Navajo and Paiute peoples make up the tribes immediately around the Can-

Not one to pass up a little fun, the Governor got involved in a "holdup" complete with a hanging. She refused to commute the sentence claiming "anyone who robs a train deserves to hang." The watch robbers "stole" from her is now in the museum.

Occasionally a special train will allow passengers the extra thrill of a photo run with all of the sights and sounds that make steam trains a joy to behold. Everyone with a camera or a recorder gets something extra to take home.

yon and have exerted the greatest influences in the immediate area. Today they are a large part of the tourist industry in and around the national park and monuments. For several tribes the canyons of the Little Colorado and Colorado rivers have deep religious significance and remain a part of their ancient culture and heritage.

Although Anglos in the persons of fur trappers and traders made their appearance in the 1820s it was not until the mid to late 1880s before they began to move onto the Colorado Plateau in ever increasing numbers. Escaping from mid-Western religious persecution the Mormon pioneers began their westward move into Utah around the Great Salt Lake in 1847. In the years immediately following their colonizing they covered virtually all of the plateau and valley regions of Utah and the high desert and forested country of northern Arizona.

Many non-Mormons began to explore and exploit this area for its mineral wealth and superb grazing lands. Large ranches sprang up in the northern Arizona country along the Mogollon Rim and in the Williams-Grand Canyon area. Cattle and sheep interests held sway in the territory for many years. Then in 1882 the Atlantic and Pacific Railroad entered and crossed Arizona on the 35th parallel.

This invasion brought with it full sized towns all along the line. And with these towns came people—all kinds of people. Some

Entertainment on the train is a regular feature. Singers, instrumental groups and Indian dancers are but a few of the variety that passengers can find on their train.

worked on the railroad and some operated stores. Others administered to their health or taught school to the kids. Prospectors poked around for valuable minerals and miners dug them out. And like the Indians who preceded them the predators who took from the less strong always made their appearance. Soldiers and marshals followed to protect people from the Indians and the lawless. Loggers cut and hauled the timber from the forests and lumber mills appeared in or near the towns to supply ties for the railroad, timber for the mines and lumber for the towns.

After many thousands of years of slow development the plateau began to change rapidly. Many different kinds of people, Irishmen, Welshmen, Mexicans, Chinese, Japanese, Germans, Finns, Swedes, Basques and Englishmen, came from all corners of the world to make their fortunes and establish homes and many of these people's descendents can still be found in the Williams-Flagstaff-Grand Canyon area today. The transition is not over. Representatives from virtually all ethnic and religious groups are still making their appearance in the search for better homes and jobs. Flagstaff is growing at a phenomenal rate and includes a major university. Williams has been static for many years but due to the tenacity of its people and return of the railroad it is again growing and some envision a population of up to eight thousand. Grand Canyon Village has reached the limits of its permanent population. Presently its tourist visitation for the year is exceeding four million annually. Maybe it is also reaching the limits of the numbers of visitors who can safely enter the Park during the summer months.

Family outings, celebrations of anniversaries, birthdays and weddings have all become a regular part of the Grand Canyon Railway.

When the train winds through the switchbacks of Coconino Canyon around MP 56 the rider is treated to several different phenomena. The curves actually turn back on themselves and the only way to keep track of it is to watch the sun. One minute it will be on the left side and in a few minutes it appears on the right. The close confines of the canyon also allows the rider to hear the echos of the steam engine as it works the grades.

Shortly after the train climbs out of Coconino Canyon the Highland Mary appears on the west side of the train. This is one of the few occupied dwellings along the line and has a history that dates back to the mining days of the Cañon. The name comes from the original mining claim.

Under a clear blue sky and the shadow of Bill Williams mountain GCRy No. 18 steams out of Williams trailing six Harriman style Pullman cars. The end of the 1989 season gave the railroad a chance to try its skills at running in the snow. Passengers enjoyed the runs with the countryside and Cañon all decorated in pristine white.

The beautiful landforms are the more permanent residents of the Grand Canyon region. People are the curiosities visited upon the environment. It will be interesting to see which of the two survives. Although humankind has in some cases managed to seriously damage the environment the safe money is on the land.

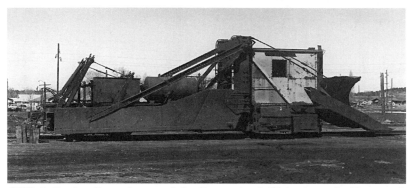

GCRy's Jordan Spreader as originally received. This piece of rolling stock is pushed along the track to clear snow with the front plow and side wings. It can also be used for spreading ballast along the right-of-way.

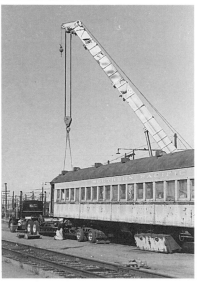

The interior of one of the SP cars brought to Tucson for overhaul. Workmen removed and replaced most of the interiors and electrical work and then painted them.

One of GCRy's cars gets a lift onto a truck at the SP Oakland yards for a trip to the shops that repaired the trucks in preparation for the trip to Williams.

Car No. 2145 makes its way through the streets of the East Bay north of Oakland enroute to Richmond. Drivers stopped their cars in traffic or chased alongside. Pedestrians froze in their tracks to stare with unbelieving eyes at the huge eighty foot long cars as they moved up the streets of the East Bay communities.

Seven cars arrive in the Pacific Fruit Express car yards at Tucson for overhaul and repainting in preparation for the re-inaugural run. The two cars behind the engine are to be painted for the Southern Pacific "Daylight" train.

Workmen put the finishing touches on the interior of a GCRy car.

A car fresh out of the PFE paint shop sports the company name.

Seven freshly painted cars arrive in the Williams yards on 10 Sep 1989.

The newly overhauled interior of the cars with its fresh paint, new woodwork and upholstery and bright brass fittings give off a real feeling of Pullman luxury.

Work continued on the cars in the company's new shop. Workers gutted the interiors, patched metal and wood, replaced windows, and then moved the cars outside to be primered and painted. They then finished the interior trim woodwork, painting and upholstery.

Number 18 in its Lake Superior& Ishpeming Railroad livery. Built by Alco in 1910 it hauled iron ore on this line until retired in 1960. It went into storage and changed hands several times and did not run again until 17 September 1989 on the Grand Canyon Railway.

Number 18's less than glamorous entrance into Williams in August, 1989. Stripped, covered with red lead paint and on the back of a 100 ton flat car she certainly looked forlorn. In little more than a month the enginemen had her completely overhauled and looking like new.

RECONSTRUCTION

When the Grand Canyon Railway announced its intent to restore steam train service from Williams to the Grand Canyon on 10 January 1989 it detailed proposed plans for construction and implied far more than simply putting a train on the existing rails. The project from the very first involved bricks and mortar along with rails, spikes and locomotives. Rehabilitation of existing equipment and facilities, and construction of maintenance shops occupied virtually every hour between 29 March and 17 September, 1989. Long range goals include light rail service within the national park, hotel expansion, a restaurant, and an RV park.

The company began rehabilitation of the right-of-way and the Fray Marcos Hotel and depot in Williams almost immediately and it located, purchased and delivered to the site specialized track equipment along with the necessary materials to complete the task. They hired track and bridge & building supervisors who in turn hired, trained and scheduled crews. Cleanup of the Fray Marcos began in preparation for repairs and restoration work. Actual physical work on the tracks and buildings began on 29 March 1989.

Obviously the tracks and bridges along the right-of-way needed considerable work to bring them into first class condition. No work had been done by the Santa Fe along the line since 1974 and thieves and the elements had exacted their toll. About 30,000 out of 225,000 ties needed to be replaced along with hundreds of rail bolts sheared off by thermal expansion and contraction of the rails. The entire line needed reballasting and several roadbed washouts required refilling due to a fifteen year lack of maintenance and water erosion. Some worn bridge timbers required replacement and abutments needed shoring up.

Consultants with years of railroad experience inspected the tracks and structures, outlined the work required and reinspected upon completion. In this manner considerable current expertise came into play without establishing a large bureaucracy. Other retired railroad men helped with advice and problem solving.

Track work began at milepost five where one mile of track had been torn up by thieves who stole the ties for resale. At least they left the ninety pound rail along with the tie plates and spikes. They remained in good shape despite the lack of attention over the years. Oddly enough the rails and fittings had a higher value than the ties but could not be disposed of as easily. This stretch of track turned out to be the training ground for the track crews who needed to learn their jobs and how to work together. Here they laid track from the ground up. The crews prepared the roadbed, placed ties, spiked tie plates in place, installed rails, bolted and spiked and finally aligned the tracks in readiness for ballast. They began work on a decrepit, out-of-service, sixty-four mile right-of-way and in five months turned it into a first class line. Hard work, a job well learned, a time to be proud.

Machines accomplished much of the heavy work while the crews did the necessary hand work. Front end loaders, hy-rail dump trucks, spike pullers and tampers all helped the crews get the job done. Tie machines took care of some of the back-breaking labor of tie removal and replacement. In the old days requirements called for a track gang of six men to pull and install eight to fifteen ties per day per man. The same number of men now do three hundred per day. Two men pulled and replaced the ties and tamped them in place using the machine while the other four replaced plates and spiked rails to the new ties using mauls and a pneumatic jack hammer. When the ballast train began operations in June two other machines moved onto the tracks to complete the process. Ballast regulators and surfacing machines made the final adjustments of tamping ballast, leveling and aligning the tracks and finishing the surface.

These crews also performed tasks other than the track work. Trees grown up during the years of inattention along the right-of-way and in the National Park yards had to be cut and removed. Because the ties had been buried for up to fifty years all of the railroad crossings needed to be completely rebuilt. In order to keep traffic problems to a minimum these men removed and replaced all six park crossings and had them ready for asphalt in two days. In compliance with state safety regulations they later installed automatic crossing gates.

Bridge and building crews had to schedule their work around the track crews because both crews could not work at the

GCRy No. 18 is lifted off the flatcar by two 200 ton cranes.

same location. Out of necessity B&B crews worked in advance of the track crews in order to have the bridge work completed before track work commenced. Most bridge beams remained in a good state of preservation as they had received thorough treatment with creosote and did not come in contact with the damp ground.

Chairman Max Biegert guides the pilot wheels of No. 18 onto the track. This is the first steam engine on these rails since 1953.

Wear and tear by years of trains passing over the bridges with resulting movement of the beams dictated replacements.

These B&B crews did much of their work using heavy hand tools such as jacks and drills with several foot long augers. Occasionally they used a Pettibone combination front-end loader and crane to maneuver the huge beams into place before drilling and installing the retaining bolts. Whatever the job required the B&B gang took care of it as a self contained unit.

While all of the track and bridge work proceeded at full speed the rehabilitation of the Fray Marcos and depot in Williams got under way and maintained the same pace. In order to have a facility for passengers in Williams the company decided to take what had become a derelict building and return it to a semblance of the centerpiece of the city it had once been. The Fray Marcos is listed on the National Register of Historic Places due to its historic past.

It is the largest and oldest remaining poured concrete building in Arizona. This turned out to be one of the greatest stumbling blocks to its rehabilitation. Virtually all of its vintage electrical and plumbing is encased within these massive walls and could not be worked on in place. New utilities had to be installed in such a manner as to not destroy the integrity and esthetics of the old facility while servicing the current needs.

Locomotives No. 19 and 20 rest on a Grand Canyon Railway siding after being unloaded.

When the company acquired the building it was derelict in every sense of the word. Vandals had made the once-posh rooms their own and decorated them with spray paint in every conceivable color and design. What they didn't paint they destroyed. Windows and doors had long since been broken and plumbing fixtures ripped from their fastenings. Even the office of the last occupant, the Santa Fe field engineer, did not escape their destruction. Just prior to his vacating the premises, the vandals broke into the office and thoroughly wrought havoc by scattering valuable documents and drawings containing years of history over the floor. To compound their wanton act, the ceiling leaked water from a heavy rain onto these irreplaceable artifacts and turned them into so much pulp. All of this material had to be sorted through for anything salvageable and the residue taken to the dump. Before restoration work could begin the debris accumulated through many years of neglect and vandalism required several days to remove.

Another unusual feature of the building caused considerable labor to remedy. Originally the hotel and depot had been designed with flat roofs by a California architect who had no concept of the magnitude of northern Arizona snowfalls. Even in the early years when well maintained by the railroad it did not take very long for

103

the building to leak like a sieve. Santa Fe engineers went to work on an inexpensive solution. Their answer to the problem included the use of readily available volcanic cinders and required tons of these to be hauled up onto the roofs and formed into peaks which they then covered with asphalt. It worked as long as the asphalt roofing received constant attention. When the railroad abandoned the buildings and maintenance ceased the cinders became a reservoir for rain and melted snow. The water trickled down through the walls and ceilings as in a living cave and inflicted grievous injury to structural members, plumbing, and electrical systems.

Core samples determined the extent of damage and repairs reclaimed the structural integrity of the buildings. In order to prevent the same situation from repeating itself the Grand Canyon Railway crews hauled small Bobcat front end loaders onto the roofs and removed the cinders. Then carpenters framed in a peaked roof and covered this with asphalt roofing. New copper scuppers for drainage assisted in the removal of water. With the structure again watertight the interior work could begin.

Installation of new public rest rooms in the old freight station facilities began along with renovation of the old waiting rooms into a new ticket counter and gift shop. The Fred Harvey dining room became the company's museum dedicated to the preservation of the cultural history of the railroad. Even the large fireplace in the old Indian room got a thorough cleaning and became the center piece of the new lounge. Workmen installed new windows designed after the originals. Sandblasting of the exterior had to go through layers of paint left cracked and peeling by years of neglect. The original 1908 layer determined the color of the renovated buildings. As soon as the sanding crews finished their chore, the painters arrived to add the touch that seemed to bring the building back to life.

By the time the 16th of September rolled around the buildings had been restored to a reasonable facsimile of their former selves and ready to receive the public. After years of neglect and frenzied restoration, the venerable structure resumed its proper place as the center of activity for the city of Williams.

Another structure required immediate attention. The mechanical department had to have a facility where it could work on engines and cars out of the weather. This construction began with a blast. Sub-surface volcanic rocks required charges of explosives to shatter them in order to enable workmen to build the foundations and drop pit of the new shop.

As soon as excavation of the site had been completed framing and the assembly of spiderwebs of reinforcing rod began in preparation for the tons of concrete required for the floors, supports and pit. Fortunately the solid footing of the malpais rock made the support necessary for the overhead crane and the tons of machinery more secure. This project became a slow process of preparation, pouring concrete and allowing it to cure before additions could be made to the building itself. Finally the steel framework appeared and metal roofing and siding began to cover the skeleton. Electrical installations for the heavy equipment and machinery required more time.

Finally in December the mechanical department began to move the tools of their trade into the shop and limited work began. But they could not utilize it fully until January due to some uncompleted construction. By the end of January engines 18 and 29 had been moved into the shop and completely stripped down in preparation for a thorough overhaul and rebuilding. In February the car department moved its first car in for interior renovation. Up until this time these crews had worked on their equipment out in the open.

For the most part these projects completed the first phase of the reconstruction and construction of the Grand Canyon Railway. Planning and work is in progress for the hotel, theme park, guest ranch, spur track to the Grand Canyon airport, and remaining shop facilities to complete this ambitious project.

Mechanics guide an overhauled piston valve into the cylinder on No. 18. All of this work had to be done out in the open as the shop was under construction. This situation allowed the public to watch the process.

GCRy No. 18 rests beneath the historic El Tovar hotel at the south rim of the Grand Canyon on 17 September 1989 after making the first steam powered trip from Williams since the early 1950s. The crowds appreciated this setting as the hotel (1905), the depot (1910), and the engine (1910) are all of the same vintage.

With a firm hand on the controls a GCRy engineer guides No. 18 out of the Grand Canyon yards for the run to Williams.

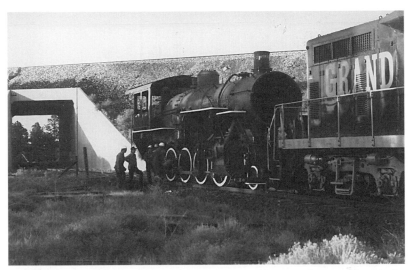

Before No. 18 could run under it's own power the running gear had to be drag tested and adjusted. Here the mechanics lubricate the bearings near the Santa Fe overpass.

After the boiler had passed it's hydrostatic testing the enginemen installed the insulation and jacket. Although much mechanical work was still required this last step then set up the engine for a new coat of paint.

Before No. 29 could enter the new shop for overhaul and rebuilding the boiler had to be thoroughly sandblasted to remove the accumulation of rust and scale built up since its last use.

Both Nos. 18 and 29 required considerable patching in the fireboxes, boilers and crown sheets. Boiler trolls replaced worn sections with such skill that the new patches are probably stronger than the originals.

LOCOMOTIVES
AND ROLLING STOCK

Through much of 1988 company management conducted searches for motive power and rolling stock. By January, 1989 several possibilities had been explored and the most likely candidates identified for inspection and possible purchase.

The first purchases came in January when the company bought seventeen coaches from the Southern Pacific Lines. These cars had been in service for their entire careers on the San Jose to San Francisco commuter run. All had been built by the Pullman Standard Company in 1923, delivered to the Bay area and put into service for the duration. Some hauled passengers for some sixty-one years before being retired to the Oakland yards in 1984.

While in storage these cars became the target of every rock chucker and transient in the area. Hardly any windows survived these years and the interiors became trash dumps and vandalized. Fires had been started in some, seats torn out, fixtures broken and the interiors generally torn up. What the vandals didn't damage the environment did. Salt air from the nearby San Francisco Bay slowly rusted out whatever metal it contacted. In short, the cars required a complete rebuilding.

Only seven of the cars survived in good enough condition to be transported over Santa Fe and Southern Pacific rails. These seven cars had been stored in a more secure area of the Oakland yards. This kept them from being constantly vandalized. The other ten had to be loaded onto flat bed trucks and hauled to the Richmond Machine & Fabricating Company in Richmond, California for repair of the trucks and couplers. On 13 January trucks and crews of the Jim Dobbas company began removing the trucks and cutting off all suspended gear such as the battery box and generator and loading them one by one onto flat beds for the journey up through the streets and cities of the East Bay. They dealt with minimal clearances and heavy traffic as though they did this every day. People stopped and stared as trucks with an eighty foot railway car in tow passed up the street. The move certainly had the atmosphere of a circus come to town.

No scheduled maintenance or inspections had been done on these cars for at least five years so the remaining seven cars required considerable work in the Oakland yards to prepare them for the move to the Pacific Fruit Express car yards in Tucson, Arizona where the company leased space for the rebuilding and contracted for sandblasting and painting. GCRy crews did the necessary maintenance and when Santa Fe and Southern Pacific inspectors passed them the cars began their journey on 9 April. However, they placed a forty mile per hour restriction on them and this necessitated travel strictly in the consist of locals. It took them five days to cover nine hundred miles. Early in the morning of 15 April the cars arrived in the SP yards at Tucson.

Later in the morning an SP switch engine moved the seven cars onto a track adjacent to the PFE shops where all of the work of rebuilding would be done except for the sandblasting and painting. Electricians, carpenters, welders, upholsterers and car men worked long, hard hours to prepare the cars for their inaugural run in September. As the days wore on the temperatures in this desert community began to climb over 100°F every day. Inside the cars it became even hotter. An adjustment to the work schedules started the crews early in the morning hours and gave them a break at the hottest part of the day.

All of the hard work paid off for at 12:45 on 10 September the Santa Fe local freight from Phoenix to Winslow dropped off seven immaculate Grand Canyon Railway passenger cars in front of the Fray Marcos Hotel and depot in Williams. Minor touchups continued on up until the 14th but the cars arrived ready for service.

Motive power for the company's roster provided a bit more anxiety and hard work than the cars. Management determined two basic types of engines had to be procured to handle the company's needs. Diesel road switchers could take care of ballast distribution and yard work but steam locomotives would be the required power for the passenger trains. It had long since been decided upon in the early days of the company that the line would be historically based using vintage equipment. Steam power answered the nostalgia requirements and the authenticity of an early 1900s passenger train from Williams to the Grand Canyon.

Double-Headed "Schoolteacher's Special" a the original Grand Canyon depot in June 1904. Engineer "Grizzly" Anderson and Fireman "Curley" Lancaster pose with their train during a stop at the Cañon enroute to the St. Louis World's Fair from Los Angeles.

Diesel road switchers did not pose a major problem. Arrangements for the purchase of two from the Santa Fe took several months and on 29 March two vintage GP-7s became the GCRy's first motive power. On 23 April Nos. 2072 and 2134 arrived at

Enginemen install a rebuilt lubricator on GCRy No. 18. Years of wear-and-tear and neglect caused many systems to deteriorate beyond repair. New replacement parts are difficult to obtain and many have to be constructed from scratch in the company shops.

Steam engines are simple systems that are built in a complicated manner. Working on one is no simple task. To access an area of the firebox several other systems have to be disconnected and reassembled once the original job is completed. Also, many tools are heavy and powerful which requires more than one man to handle them.

Williams on the local from Cleburne, Texas. As they had not been serviced for some weeks it took several days to prepare them but on 26 April at 5:32 PM both engines moved onto Grand Canyon Railway tracks under their own power. No engine had done so since the last Santa Fe work extra on 20 June 1974.

Some steam purists might say these engines have no business being on the line but the record indicates otherwise. Steam locomotives ran the line in regular service from 1900 to 1953 and diesels from 1951 to 1974. Two EMC E-2 diesels actually made an appearance at the Canyon in 1938 on inaugural runs of the Santa Fe Chief and El Capitan. GP-7s of the 2650 class saw passenger service on the line for several years in the 1950s. Both 2072 and 2134 are of the original high nose 2650 class but have been rebuilt and renumbered by the Santa Fe at the Cleburne, Texas shops in the 1970s. Numbers 2072 and 2134 currently are of the Santa Fe 2050 class. At any rate these two engines are historically appropriate.

Engine 2134 is the younger of the two having been built by EMD in November, 1953 with builder's number 18898 and Santa Fe's road number 2881. Number 2072 came off the line in December, 1953 as Santa Fe 2888 with builder's number 18905. In June, 1974 No. 2888 left the Cleburne shops after a complete

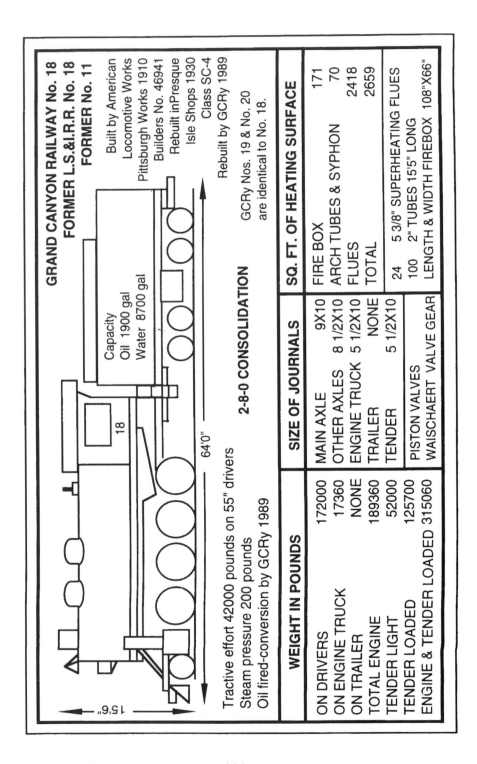

GRAND CANYON RAILWAY No. 18
FORMER L.S.&I.R.R. No. 18
FORMER No. 11

Built by American
Locomotive Works
Pittsburgh Works 1910
Builders No. 46941
Rebuilt inPresque
Isle Shops 1930
Class SC-4

Rebuilt by GCRy 1989

GCRy Nos. 19 & No. 20
are identical to No. 18.

Capacity
Oil 1900 gal
Water 8700 gal

2-8-0 CONSOLIDATION

Tractive effort 42000 pounds on 55" drivers
Steam pressure 200 pounds
Oil fired-conversion by GCRy 1989

18

64'0"

15'6"

WEIGHT IN POUNDS

ON DRIVERS	172000
ON ENGINE TRUCK	17360
ON TRAILER	NONE
TOTAL ENGINE	189360
TENDER LIGHT	52000
TENDER LOADED	125700
ENGINE & TENDER LOADED	315060

SIZE OF JOURNALS

MAIN AXLE	9X10
OTHER AXLES	8 1/2X10
ENGINE TRUCK	5 1/2X10
TRAILER	NONE
TENDER	5 1/2X10

PISTON VALVES
WAISCHAERT VALVE GEAR

SQ. FT. OF HEATING SURFACE

FIRE BOX	171
ARCH TUBES & SYPHON	70
FLUES	2418
TOTAL	2659

24   5 3/8" SUPERHEATING FLUES
100   2" TUBES 15'5" LONG
LENGTH & WIDTH FIREBOX 108"X66"

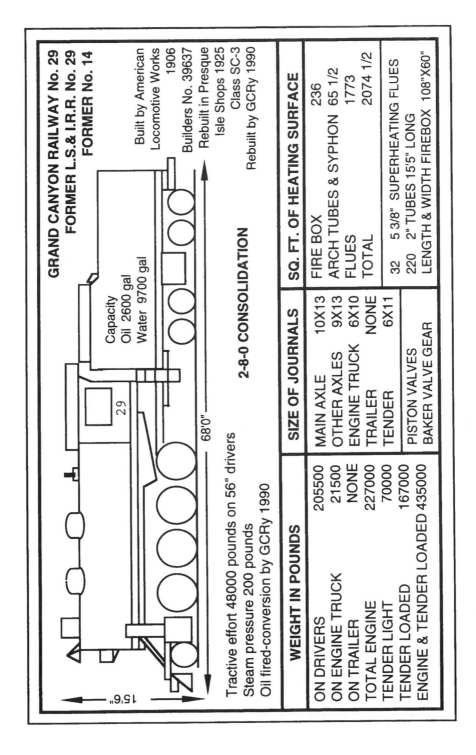

GRAND CANYON RAILWAY No. 29
FORMER L.S.& I.R.R. No. 29
FORMER No. 14

Built by American
Locomotive Works
1906
Builders No. 39637
Rebuilt in Presque
Isle Shops 1925
Class SC-3
Rebuilt by GCRy 1990

Capacity
Oil 2600 gal
Water 9700 gal

2-8-0 CONSOLIDATION

68'0"

29

15'6"

Tractive effort 48000 pounds on 56" drivers
Steam pressure 200 pounds
Oil fired-conversion by GCRy 1990

WEIGHT IN POUNDS

ON DRIVERS	205500
ON ENGINE TRUCK	21500
ON TRAILER	NONE
TOTAL ENGINE	227000
TENDER LIGHT	70000
TENDER LOADED	167000
ENGINE & TENDER LOADED	435000

SIZE OF JOURNALS

MAIN AXLE	10X13
OTHER AXLES	9X13
ENGINE TRUCK	6X10
TRAILER	NONE
TENDER	6X11
PISTON VALVES	
BAKER VALVE GEAR	

SQ. FT. OF HEATING SURFACE

FIRE BOX	236
ARCH TUBES & SYPHON	65 1/2
FLUES	1773
TOTAL	2074 1/2

32   5 3/8" SUPERHEATING FLUES
220 2" TUBES 15'5" LONG
LENGTH & WIDTH FIREBOX 108"X60"

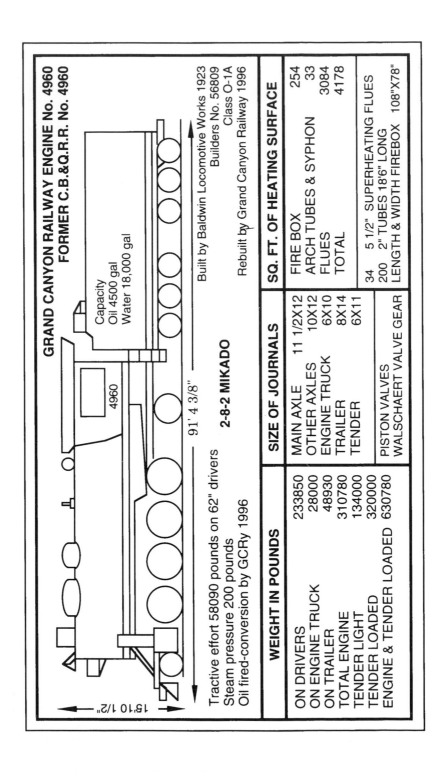

GRAND CANYON RAILWAY ENGINE No. 4960
FORMER C.B.&Q.R.R. No. 4960

2-8-2 MIKADO

4960

91' 4 3/8"

13'10 1/2"

Capacity
Oil 4500 gal
Water 18,000 gal

Built by Baldwin Locomotive Works 1923
Builders No. 56809
Class O-1A

Rebuilt by Grand Canyon Railway 1996

Tractive effort 58090 pounds on 62" drivers
Steam pressure 200 pounds
Oil fired-conversion by GCRy 1996

WEIGHT IN POUNDS

ON DRIVERS	233850
ON ENGINE TRUCK	28000
ON TRAILER	48930
TOTAL ENGINE	310780
TENDER LIGHT	134000
TENDER LOADED	320000
ENGINE & TENDER LOADED	630780

SIZE OF JOURNALS

MAIN AXLE	11 1/2X12
OTHER AXLES	10X12
ENGINE TRUCK	6X10
TRAILER	8X14
TENDER	6X11

PISTON VALVES
WALSCHAERT VALVE GEAR

SQ. FT. OF HEATING SURFACE

FIRE BOX	254
ARCH TUBES & SYPHON	33
FLUES	3084
TOTAL	4178

34   5 1/2" SUPERHEATING FLUES
200 2" TUBES 186" LONG
LENGTH & WIDTH FIREBOX   108"X78"

116

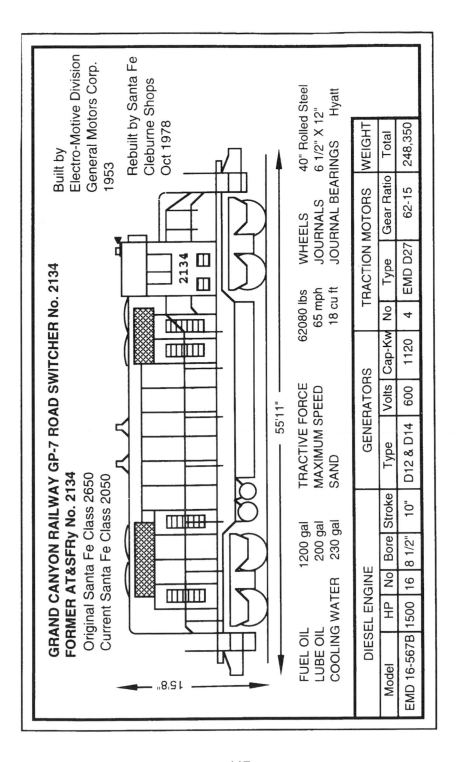

GRAND CANYON RAILWAY GP-7 ROAD SWITCHER No. 2134
FORMER AT&SFRy No. 2134
Original Santa Fe Class 2650
Current Santa Fe Class 2050

Built by
Electro-Motive Division
General Motors Corp.
1953

Rebuilt by Santa Fe
Cleburne Shops
Oct 1978

FUEL OIL 1200 gal
LUBE OIL 200 gal
COOLING WATER 230 gal

TRACTIVE FORCE 62080 lbs
MAXIMUM SPEED 65 mph
SAND 18 cu ft

WHEELS 40" Rolled Steel
JOURNALS 6 1/2" X 12"
JOURNAL BEARINGS Hyatt

55'11"
15'8"

2134

DIESEL ENGINE				
Model	HP	No	Bore	Stroke
EMD 16-567B	1500	16	8 1/2"	10"

GENERATORS		
Type	Volts	Cap-Kw
D12 & D14	600	1120

TRACTION MOTORS		
No	Type	Gear Ratio
4	EMD D27	62-15

WEIGHT
Total
248,350

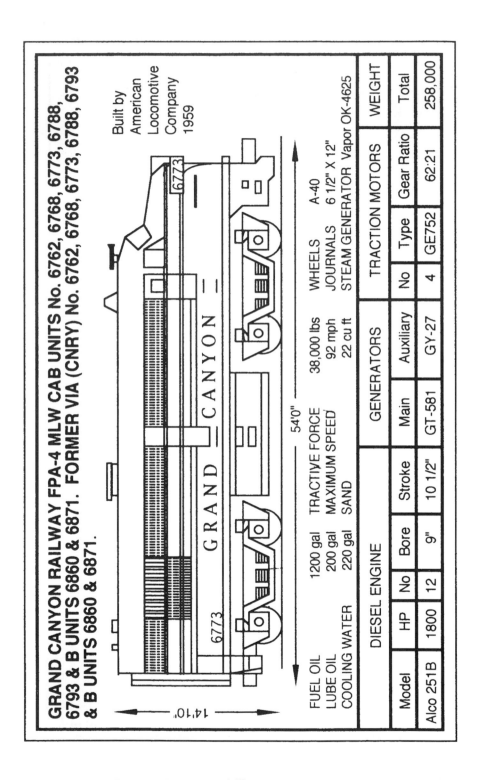

GRAND CANYON RAILWAY FPA-4 MLW CAB UNITS No. 6762, 6768, 6773, 6788, 6793 & B UNITS 6860 & 6871. FORMER VIA (CNRY) No. 6762, 6768, 6773, 6788, 6793 & B UNITS 6860 & 6871.

Built by
American
Locomotive
Company
1959

GRAND CANYON

6773

6773

14'10"

54'0"

FUEL OIL	1200 gal	TRACTIVE FORCE	38,000 lbs
LUBE OIL	200 gal	MAXIMUM SPEED	92 mph
COOLING WATER	220 gal	SAND	22 cu ft

WHEELS	A-40
JOURNALS	6 1/2" X 12"
STEAM GENERATOR	Vapor OK-4625

DIESEL ENGINE

Model	HP	No	Bore	Stroke
Alco 251B	1800	12	9"	10 1/2"

GENERATORS

Main	Auxiliary
GT-581	GY-27

TRACTION MOTORS

No	Type	Gear Ratio
4	GE752	62:21

WEIGHT

Total
258,000

118

GRAND CANYON RAILWAY F40FH Nos. 237, 239 & 295.
FORMER AMTRAK F40PH NOS. 237, 239 & 295.

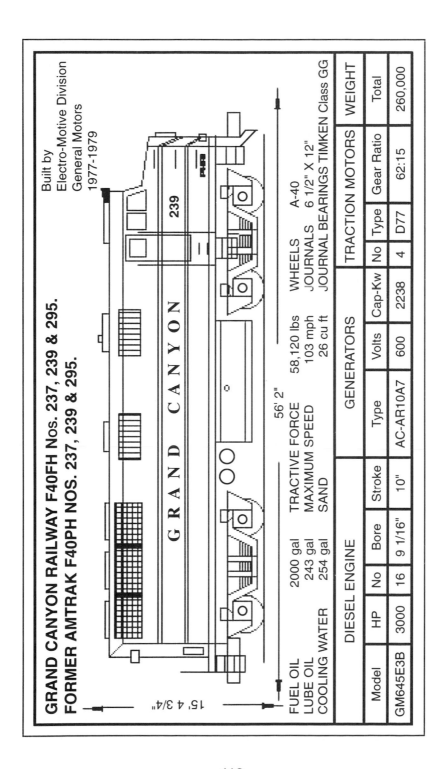

GRAND CANYON 239

Built by
Electro-Motive Division
General Motors
1977-1979

56' 2"

15' 4 3/4"

FUEL OIL   2000 gal   TRACTIVE FORCE   58,120 lbs   WHEELS   A-40
LUBE OIL   243 gal   MAXIMUM SPEED   103 mph   JOURNALS   6 1/2" X 12"
COOLING WATER   254 gal   SAND   26 cu ft   JOURNAL BEARINGS TIMKEN Class GG

DIESEL ENGINE

Model	HP	No	Bore	Stroke
GM645E3B	3000	16	9 9/16"	10"

GENERATORS

Type	Volts	Cap-Kw
AC-AR10A7	600	2238

TRACTION MOTORS

No	Type	Gear Ratio
4	D77	62:15

WEIGHT

Total
260,000

rebuilding as 2072. No. 2881 did not complete the rebuilding until October, 1978 and entered service as 2134. This accounts for the younger engine having a higher number. When originally built both of these locomotives came equipped with dynamic brakes and steam generators for passenger service. Neither are so configured today. This need for a steam generator on the diesels resulted in the sale of 2072 in 1991 with the subsequent purchase of an Alco FPA-4 unit from VIA (Canadian National Railway). No. 6773 is equipped with a steam generator and of a similar type once in service with the Santa Fe on this line.

Finding steam locomotives in reasonably good condition became a real problem for the company. The operations department rejected many offers of sale due to the terrible condition of the equipment or they found them inappropriate for use on the Grand Canyon line. Other engines would have made good additions to the company roster but could not be bought at any price. Equipment from all over the United States, Canada, Mexico and finally even China came under scrutiny. Due to every conceivable reason the search narrowed down to a very few possibilities.

In April two company representatives traveled to China in order to inspect several American made Baldwin locomotives. Built in 1947 and shipped to China, they have been in continual service on their national railways. Negotiations for the purchase and shipment of four KD-7s did not take long to run into the bureaucratic loggerheads common in the Chinese system. While discussions continued students in China began to demonstrate for more freedoms. The massacre at Tiananmen Square created a situation the owner could not abide with. He cancelled negotiations, returned to the United States, and decided the company would buy American.

At this juncture it became necessary to make an immediate purchase of motive power or the company would not be able to make its commitment of running a steam train on the 88th anniversary of the first scheduled train from Williams to the Grand Canyon on 17 September. Thus the decision to purchase four 1906-1910 vintage American Locomotive Company (Alco) 2-8-0 Consolidation type locomotives. These had run all of their useful life hauling iron ore on the Lake Superior & Ishpeming Railroad in Michigan.

The company completed purchase agreements with John Slack in July. He had purchased numbers 18, 19 and 20 for use on his Lake States Steam Transportation Company at Laona, Wisconsin. Slack moved No. 18 to Laona and left both Nos. 19 and 20 at the LS&I in Marquette. Steve Mattox of Council Bluffs, Iowa

Overhaul of a steam engine requires a detailed disassembly and provides a rare opportunity to see the interior fixtures in the smoke box. The large holes in the front flue sheet are for the superheater tubes and the smaller holes are the actual flues. This view also allows a look through the steam valves just above the pilot on both sides.

purchased No. 29 and moved it to the Mid-Continent Railroad Museum at North Freedom, Wisconsin. When approached by the GCRy he agreed to sell.

Alco built all four locomotives for the LS&I. Of these, No. 29 is the oldest and largest. They saw continual service hauling iron ore to the docks of Marquette, Michigan from their date of delivery

After completion of extensive boiler work, No. 29 waits for reassembly of the superheater units.

until 1960. All had been completely rebuilt at company shops in 1930. The LS&I retired all four in 1960 and sold them to the Marquette and Huron Mountain Railroad for use on a scenic line in the area. Of the four only number 19 saw any service on the railroad and the others remained in storage until sold to Slack and Mattox in 1985.

Crews scrambled to Laona and Marquette in July to prepare the engines and tenders for movement to Williams. Time was running out. The Santa Fe had the only available 100 ton flat cars needed to transport all of this equipment and they were not immediately forthcoming. Selected to make the inaugural run on 17 September, mechanics used this time to accomplish some work on No. 18. Finally the cars arrived and cranes loaded the four locomotives for the speedy trip to Arizona. But due to delays caused by the Chicago & Northwestern No. 18 did not arrive in Williams until 20 August. Numbers 19, 20 and four tenders arrived seven days later and finally on the 30th No. 29 showed up.

To lift the engines from the cars to the tracks required two 200 ton cranes. As one of these needed to travel 180 miles from Phoenix for the job the mechanical department decided to wait until all four engines arrived before ordering the crane. For eleven days enginemen worked feverishly on No. 18 perched high in the air on the flat car. On 31 August the cranes set up on a GCRy siding in full view of downtown Williams and began the process of unloading. The tenders for Numbers 18 and 29 became the first to be lifted free of the flat cars. Then at 12:17 PM on a cloudless and spectacularly clear day, No. 18 slowly cleared the flat and settled gently to the waiting rails. The first steam engine since 1953 to rest on Grand Canyon Railway tracks. Although stripped down and wearing a shabby coat of rust she looked beautiful to everyone waiting years for this day. No cheers—mostly quiet congratulations and relief was the order of the day for the spectators and railway personnel. By the end of the day the diesels had shuffled all of the cars into place while the crane crews gently placed each piece of equipment on the tracks.

The steam locomotives finally arrived but now only seventeen days remained until the first scheduled passenger train of the new railroad must leave the station on its run. Much work still remained to be done; finish the boiler work, overhaul pistons and running gear, convert the engine from coal to oil burning systems, rebuild the tender to carry oil instead of coal, inspect and repair pumps, manufacture dozens of new parts, install new insulation and jacket, polish and hang the jewelry (bell and whistle), and finally give it a new coat of shiny black paint with red and white trim. How could all of this be done in the short time remaining?

Enginemen, mechanics and other company personnel, family and friends worked eighteen and twenty hour days in order to make up for lost time. The tasks which required the skill gained in years of working on steam equipment had to be left to those with the knowledge. Willing and less skilled workers handled the other jobs such as painting and some of the general wrench bending. Everyone had a goal and worked steadily toward it. On 8 September the diesels coupled onto No. 18 and began drag testing of the running gear. Several runs as far out as MP 3.8 gave people a chance to see what a steam engine on the main line looked like even if it wasn't under its own power.

Work continued out in the open almost around the clock. The company's new engine and car facility would not be completed until December. Thankfully the weather cooperated with only chilly and occasionally windy weather. On 13 September workers completed the boiler work, attached the tender and filled it with water and fuel oil. At 8:19 PM the company chairman lit the first fire in No. 18 since 1960. By the next day pressure had built up, adjustments made and the people of Williams heard something absent since 1953—the melodious sound of a whistle on a steam locomotive. It brought people from all over town. They had a railroad again!

With only four days left much remained to be done. Air connections still needed to be completed along with a thousand inspections and checks. By the evening of 16 September No. 18 still had not moved from the makeshift engine yard. A small crowd of people gathered around the outside of the fence to keep vigil. While the enginemen worked, a company-sponsored barbeque party hosted over a thousand guests in a circus tent near the Fray Marcos. People wandered back and forth between the party and the engine in hopes of seeing it run. They waited in vain for the most part. When the party finished most went home. Only the diehards remained.

At 1:23 AM of 17 September No. 18 did something no steam engine had done for thirty-six years. She moved out onto the Grand Canyon Railway main line under her own power. Barely ten and one half hours remained to test and adjust her before the reinaugural run to the Canyon. Enginemen made trial runs out as far as Red Lake with numerous stops for inspections and adjustments until the wee hours of the morning. Finally, with dawn streaking the horizon they called a halt. Except for some minor considerations the remainder could wait until later. Everyone was exhausted. They needed some rest. At least the engineer and fireman for the day's run got a full night's sleep.

By ten AM the crowds had begun to gather under glowering skies and an occasional drizzle for the day's festivities. Bands played, a cannon boomed, speakers speeched, cameras clicked and whirred and the people glanced furtively down the track. Where was the locomotive? The cars sat ready to accept their eager pas-

Number 4960 in Chiago, Burlington & Quincy livery. Completely rebuilt by the Grand Canyon Railway in its shops for service in 1996, this 2-8-2 Mikado type locomotive went through the most extensive overhaul in modern steam history

John Gruber photo

sengers but No. 18 still sat in the yard, smoke lazily spiraling up from the stack. Finally, with two short signals on the whistle, she moved out onto the main track and stopped. Billows of steam rushed from both sides of the engine as the crew blew down the boiler. Three more short signals and "The Little Engine That Could" began to back toward the station. The crowd cheered and gathered around to see the first coupling of the locomotive with the cars.

Grand Canyon Railway's reinaugural went down to the wire but the people of the railroad had done it. The day would not be without its problems but at 12:00 noon on 17 September 1989 as scheduled, the train pulled out of Williams station bound for the Grand Canyon with five cars full of jubilant passengers ready for a long celebration. Enroute No. 18 experienced some injector problems and required assistance from the diesels on the Apex grade. The delays did not dampen the spirits of the riders for they had a real party going.

While the crews handled their problems a crowd of over one thousand waited, and waited at the Canyon depot. Park Service personnel kept advising them of the train's progress over a public address system and they continued to wait. Finally the whistle could be heard at distant grade crossings. The crowd came to life and was not disappointed when the first steam train since 1953 rounded curve number 111 and eased into the yards under her own power with bell clanging and whistle blowing. The passengers detrained and gathered around the reviewing stand for the official Park Service welcome. At this dedication more dignitaries spoke to the deeds at hand, presented awards, and drove a golden spike into a tie in front of the engine.

With the day nearly complete, the train had to return to Williams. But this time it would be under diesel power for No. 18 needed repairs on a tender journal and the injector. She remained overnight on the tail of the wye while enginemen worked to have her serviceable for the next day's run. When the train arrived at noon on the 18th the crews had completed work on No. 18. She again took the lead with the diesels in trail and brought the train home to Williams.

Grand Canyon Railway's people accomplished a Herculean task under adverse conditions and the railroad maintained a regular weekend schedule through the New Year. Meanwhile work continued on the rebuilding of No. 29 and procurement of other locomotives.

On 30 August, the day before the unloading of the engines and tenders in Williams, the GCRy added another locomotive to its roster. Number 4960 is a 2-8-2 Mikado type built by Baldwin's Philadelphia works in 1923. It operated in freight service with the Chicago, Burlington and Quincy Railroad until 1960. In 1961 she entered the shops at Galesburg for a complete overhaul. Fit for service again, the CB&Q used 4960 several times in the early 1960s to haul excursion trains in the Chicago and Galesburg area where she gained the nickname "The Teacher" because of all the school children who rode behind her. Another excursion in 1963 to Casper, Wyoming resulted in 4960 being painted gold. This trip celebrated the fiftieth (golden) anniversary of service to that city.

In 1965 and 1966 she gained considerable notoriety by being the engine assigned to pull the Schlitz Circus Train around the Chicago and Milwaukee area. When maintenance costs became too great the CB&Q retired 4960 and donated her to the Circus World Museum in Baraboo, Wisconsin where she remained until donated to the Mid-Continent Railway Historical Society's museum at North Freedom, Wisconsin in the early 1970s. Mid-Continent displayed 4960 until 1982 when they decided to lease her to an excursion operator in Bristol, Virginia. Brought to Ft. Wayne, Indiana in 1985, 4960 declined in storage until purchased by the GCRy.

Mechanics began work on 4960 at Ft. Wayne. They disassembled most of the components and shipped the running gear on trucks and the remainder on flat cars. After arrival in Williams in May the locomotive rested in storage until 1994. The subject of the most extensive and complete rebuilding of a steam locomotive in modern times, No. 4960 will join the livery of Grand Canyon Railway motive power for service in 1996.

The cars from Richmond finally arrived in Williams on 3 October. Restoration work began immediately on a spur track in the work area. By December all had been gutted, sand blasted and primer painted. In January the new shop accepted the first of these cars for rebuilding of the interior. For the first time the car crews worked out of the weather. Thankfully the winter had not been severe and snow did not make a regular appearance until 29 December. With the shops in service the crews could now work without consideration for the weather.

In January, 1990 the GCRy acquired No. 324, a 1915 vintage Jordan Spreader from the Kennecott Copper Company. It operated from August, 1915 as No. 4 on their Bingham & Garfield Railway and serviced the right-of-way and tailings dumps for the open pit copper mine located southwest of Salt Lake City, Utah. While there Kennecott used it in snow removal, ballast spreading and ore dump spreading operations. The Jordan with its deep "V" plow arrived at Williams via flat bed truck on 7 March. Its primary purpose is to remove heavy snow from the right-of-way between Williams and the Grand Canyon. Without any power of its own, the unit requires either a steam or diesel locomotive to move it and supply it with compressed air for operation of its plow and wings. A complete overhaul and rebuilding in the company shop returned it to like-new condition. Quite an odd looking piece of equipment, the black and yellow Jordan can be seen on one of the company's sidings as the train arrives and departs Williams.

In 1992, the GCRy added the Chief Keokuck parlor car to its roster. Built by Pullman in 1927, the Chief is the line's most luxurious coach. Complete with kitchen and observation platform, its drawing room is furnished with comfortable chairs and couches to provide elegant accommodations for up to thirty people in the style of years gone by. Passengers have the choice of riding in air conditioned comfort or stepping out onto the rear platform for a breath of fresh pine scented air.

Also in 1992, Club Car number 2152 went into service after a complete overhaul in the company shops. Carpenters and craftsmen converted the coach into a comfortable upscale car complete with mahogany bar. Seating sixty passengers, the Club provides exceptional service with a bartender and attendant to help make the trip more enjoyable.

The railroad has a growing assortment of rolling stock and equipment that allows it to service equipment and maintain the network of track in first class condition. A fleet of tank and ballast cars transport treated water to the Grand Canyon for servicing locomotives and to handle the continuing needs of renewing ballast along the right-of-way and in the yards, and a flat car hauls rails, ties, and other equipment for maintenance of way projects. The stable of track equipment includes a ballast regulator, tamper, torsion beam tamper, scarifier, bridge crane, and two tie renewers. Also, several hy-rail equipped trucks provide maintenance crews with mobility on and off the rails to sites in the the company's yards and along the sixty-four mile right-of-way.

Looking to the future, a variety of motive power and cars are being considered for service on the GCRy. They will add to the vintage flavor of the line and provide passengers with a nostalgic return to the heyday of steam and diesel powered railroads.

WHISTLE SIGNALS

      Morse code is a series of dots and dashes representing different letters of the alphabet. Used in combination they allow telegraphers to communicate over great distances. Long before the use of radios the railroads developed a similar system for the use of engineers to communicate train movements and directions to train crew members and provide for general warning signals. As with Morse code the whistle signals are in dots and dashes represented by short and long sounds on the whistle. All telegraphers could be recognized by their "fist" or style of sending. Locomotive engineers also have their individual style yet all conform to the basic code.

In the following list of signals used on the Grand Canyon Railway

    o   represents short sounds

    —   represents longer sounds

   — —   represents extra long sounds

o	Apply brakes. Stop.
— —	Release brakes. Proceed.
o o o	When standing, back. When running, stop at next station.
— —	Approaching station. Stopped at station.
— — o — —	Approaching public crossings at grade, at curves, tunnels and other obscured places; to be prolonged until crossing is reached.
— — o	General warning when approaching point engineer's view is obscured.
o o o o	Call for signals
o o —	Answer for any signal not otherwise provided for.

129

▬ o o o	Flagman protect rear of train.
o o o ▬	Flagman protect front of train.
▬ ▬ ▬ ▬	Flagman return from south (west)
▬ ▬ ▬ ▬ ▬	Flagman return from north (east)
o o ▬ ▬	Engineer on second locomotive assume control of air brakes.
o ▬	Inspect train for air line leak or for brakes sticking.
▬ ▬ ▬ o o o	Call for section men.

A series of rapid short sounds is used as a warning or attention getter for livestock or people on the right-of-way.

An extra long sound or series of extra long sounds also serves as an attention getter for passengers. i.e. departure is imminent.

STEAM LOCOMOTIVE TYPE NAMES
BY WHEEL CONFIGURATION

Wheel configuration determines a type of steam locomotive. The numbers refer to how many wheels are in the different sets. Front wheels are referred to as pony trucks and guide the engine along the rails. Drivers in the middle are the largest and provide a transfer of power from the engine to the rails. Trailing trucks at the rear support the weight of the firebox. Mallet types are articulated with two sets of drivers, hence a configuration of 2-8-8-2.

Grand Canyon Railway's No. 18 is a Consolidation type locomotive because it has a wheel configuration of 2-8-0. This means it has two wheels on the pony truck at the front, eight drivers in the middle and no trailing truck at the rear. GCRy No. 4960 is a 2-8-2 Mikado or "Mike" because it has two wheels on the trailing truck along with the two on the pony truck and eight drivers.

The following list provides the reader with a handy guide to steam locomotive types.

4-4-0	ooOO	AMERICAN
4-6-0	ooOOO	TEN WHEEL
2-8-0	oOOOO	CONSOLIDATION
2-6-0	oOOO	MOGUL
4-8-0	ooOOOO	TWELVE WHEEL
2-6-2	oOOOo	PRAIRIE
2-8-2	oOOOOo	MIKADO
2-10-0	oOOOOO	DECAPOD

2-10-2	oOOOOOo	SANTA FE
4-4-2	ooOOo	ATLANTIC
4-6-2	ooOOOo	PACIFIC
2-6-6-2	oOOO OOOo	MALLET
4-6-6-4	ooOOO OOOoo	
4-4-6-2	ooOO OOOo	
2-8-8-2	oOOOO OOOOo	
2-10-10-2	oOOOOO OOOOOo	
4-8-2	ooOOOOo	MOUNTAIN
4-6-4	ooOOOoo	HUDSON
4-8-4	ooOOOOoo	NORTHERN
2-8-4	oOOOOoo	BERKSHIRE
2-10-4	oOOOOOoo	TEXAS

BIBLIOGRAPHY

CORRESPONDENCE AND INTERVIEWS

AMBROSE, Wilfred, G., Engineering Consultant, Phoenix, Arizona.

ARIZONA BUREAU OF GEOLOGY AND MINERAL TECHNOLOGY, Geological Survey Branch, Tucson, Arizona.

ARIZONA PUBLIC SERVICE COMPANY, Flagstaff, Arizona.

BIEGERT, Max L., Chairman and Chief Executive Officer, Grand Canyon Railway, Williams, Arizona.

BLACK MESA PIPELINE COMPANY, Flagstaff, Arizona.

BLAIR, Cherrie L., Rancher, Valle, Arizona.

BLAIR, David F., Rancher, Valle, Arizona.

BOGDEN, William, Maintenance Superintendent, Kennecott Copper Company, Bingham Canyon, Utah.

CHAPPELL, Gordon, S., National Park Service Western Region Historian, San Francisco, California.

CURRY, George G., Atchison, Topeka and Santa Fe Railway Field Engineer, Williams, Arizona.

EL PASO NATURAL GAS COMPANY, El Paso, Texas.

ETCHEGARY, Sam, Rancher, Howard Lake, Arizona.

FRANZEN, Robert C., Chief Mechanical Officer, Grand Canyon Railway, Williams, Arizona.

GUEISSAZ, Erik, Highland Mary owner, Grand Canyon, Arizona.

GUEISSAZ, Sue Hovey, Highland Mary owner, Grand Canyon, Arizona.

HAYES, Charles, Pandrol/Jackson Inc., Ludington, Michigan.

LaCIVITA, Robert, Vice-president Operations, Grand Canyon Railway, Williams, Arizona.

MACAULEY, Michael P., Rancher, Flagstaff, Arizona.

MARTIN, Michael A., Burlington Notheren Santa Fe Railway, Former Manager of Public Affairs, Fort Worth, Texas.

MENNINGER, Constance L., Santa Fe Archivist, Kansas State Historical Society, Topeka, Kansas.

MILLER, Gary E., Former Car Shop Superintendent, Grand Canyon Railway, Williams, Arizona.

MORRIS, John J., Former Roadmaster, Grand Canyon Railway, Williams, Arizona.

PAGE, Larry E., Railroad Historian, Dallas, Texas.

PLESE, Sonny J., Atchison, Topeka and Santa Fe Railway Engineering Technician, Winslow, Arizona.

PLESE, Sonny J., Atchison, Topeka and Santa Fe Railway
        Engineering Technician, Winslow, Arizona.
RAMSEY, Michael D., Former Trainmaster, Grand Canyon
        Railway, Williams, Arizona.
REESE, Bryan, Former Manager of Passenger Cars, Grand
        Canyon Railway, Williams, Arizona.
RIKER, David F, Burlington Northern Santa Fe Railway
        Assistant to the Superintendent, Albuquerque
        Division, Winslow, Arizona.
TRANSWESTERN PIPELINE COMPANY, Bellemont, Arizona.
WHITE, Ervin H., Trainmaster, Grand Canyon Railway,
        Williams, Arizona.
WINGFIELD, Louis, Rancher, Willaha, Arizona.
YRIGOYEN, Sandra, Rancher, Howard Lake, Arizona.
ZICOPOULOS, Karl V., Shop Foeman, Grand Canyon
        Railway, Williams, Arizona

PUBLICATIONS AND DOCUMENTS

ATCHISON, TOPEKA AND SANTA FE RAILWAY, 1897-1953.
        Contracts, correspondence, maps, engineering drawings
        and documents. Topeka: Office of the Secretar Treasurer
CHRONIC, Halka, 1989. *Roadside Geology of Arizona.*
        Missoula: Mountain Press Publishing.
COCONINO COUNTY RECORDER. Flagstaff, Arizona.
COLLIER, Michael, 1980. *An Introduction to Grand Canyon
        Geology.* Grand Canyon: Grand Canyon Natural History
        Association.
FUCHS, James R., 1953. *A History of Williams, Arizona
        1876-1951.* University of Arizona Bulletin #23. Tucson.
GALLIZIOLI, Steve, 1979. *Discover Arizona Wildlife.*
        Phoenix: Arizona Highways.
GRAND CANYON RAILWAY, 1990. *Timetable No. 3.*
        Williams: Operating Department.
GRUBER, John, 1989. *Focus on Rails.* North Freedom:
        Mid-Continent Railway Historical Society.
KANSAS STATE HISTORICAL SOCIETY, Topeka, Kansas.
LANE, N. Gary, 1978. *Life of the Past.* Columbus: Merrill
        Publishing.
LOWE, Charles, H. (ed.) 1964. *The Vertebrates of Arizona.*
        Tucson: University of Arizona.
MANNS, Timothy, 1978. *A Guide to Grand Canyon Village
        Historic District.* Grand Canyon: Grand Canyon
        Natural History Association.

McMILLAN, Joe, 1985. *Santa Fe Motive Power*. Woodridge:
    McMillan Publications.
MUSEUM OF NORTHERN ARIZONA, Flagstaff, Arizona.
NATIONS, J. D. and STUMP, Edmund, 1981. *Geology of
    Arizona*. Dubuque: Kendall/Hunt.
NORTHERN ARIZONA UNIVERSITY, Cline Library Special
    Collections.
RICHMOND, Albert J. Jr., 1987. *Historic Precipitation
    Sequences on the Colorado Plateau, 1859-1983*. MS
    Thesis, Northern Arizona University.
SMITH, Jack, 1984. *Tales of the Beale Road*. Flagstaff: Tales
    of the Beale Road Publishing Company.
UNITED STATES DEPARTMENT OF AGRICULTURE, 1987.
    *Environmental Impact Statement for the Kaibab
    National Forest Plan*. Williams: Kaibab National Forest.
WAESCHE, Hugh, 1933. "The Anita Copper Mine." *Grand
    Canyon Nature Notes,* 7:108-112.
WAY, Thomas E., 1980. *Summary of Travel to the Grand
    Canyon*. Prescott: Prescott Graphics.
WHITE, John H. Jr., 1978. *The American Railroad Passenger
    Car*. Baltimore: Johns Hopkins University Press.
WHITNEY, Stephen, 1982. *A Field Guide to the Grand
    Canyon*. New York: Quill.
WORLEY, E. Dale, 1976. *Iron Horses of the Santa Fe Trail*.
    Dallas: Phillip M. Dybvig, Inc.

ADDITIONAL PHOTOGRAPHS

BIEGERT, Max
GRUBER, John
MID-CONTINENT RAILWAY HISTORICAL SOCIETY, North
    Freedom, Wisconsin.
NAVAJO COUNTY HISTORICAL SOCIETY, Old Trails
    Museum, Winslow, Arizona

MAPS

UNITED STATES DEPARTMENT OF AGRICULTURE, Soil
    Conservation Service, General Soil Map, Coconino
    County, Arizona, 1972, supplemented with author's data
    from personal inspection.
UNITED STATES GEOLOGICAL SURVEY topographic maps
    of Williams, Valle and Grand Canyon, Arizona, 1983 and
    1984, supplemented with author's data from personal
    inspection.

Additional copies of the Grand Canyon Railway milepost guide

RAILS TO THE RIM

copies of the Grand Canyon Railway history

COWBOYS, MINERS,
PRESIDENTS AND KINGS;
THE STORY OF THE GRAND
CANYON RAILWAY

and copies of the color pictoral history

THE GRAND CANYON RAILWAY;
SIXTY YEARS IN COLOR

may be ordered from:

GRAND CANYON RAILWAY GIFT SHOP
1201 W. ROUTE 66, SUITE 200
FLAGSTAFF, AZ 86001

COST: $9.95 each for the guide; $15.95 (soft cover) and $19.95 (hardcover) each for the history; $29.95 each for the color history; plus $5.00 each for postage and handling. Arizona residents please add 8% sales tax.